11.95

1991-

M000280239

PLA
ASPECTS
• F • R • O • M •
CONFLICT
• T • O •
COOPERATION
Tracy Marks

Making Your
Stressful Aspects
Work For You

CRCS PUBLICATIONS
Post Office Box 1460
Sebastopol, California 95472

ACKNOWLEDGMENTS: Special thanks to Jan Sahlstrom, Marie Burack, Donna Levreault, Heidi Ruthchild and David Perloff for their typing, editorial, artistic and mailing assistance; Bil Tierney for his work on the t-square configuration; the several dozen people who answered my research requests; and my parents, the Authors League Fund and the Carnegie Fund for Authors, whose financial assistance helped make this book possible.

Library of Congress Cataloging-in-Publication Data

Marks, Tracy, 1950–
  Planetary aspects.

  Rev. ed. of: How to handle your T-square. c1979.
  Bibliography: p.
  1. Astrology. I. Marks, Tracy, 1950–
How to handle your T-square. II. Title.
BF1708.1.M373 1987   133.5   86-26445
ISBN 0-916360-32-6 (pbk.)
Revised edition, formerly titled *How to Handle Your T-Square*, newly titled
Planetary Aspects: From Conflict to Cooperation

INTERNATIONAL STANDARD BOOK NUMBER: 0-916360-32-6

Published simultaneously in the United States and Canada by:
CRCS Publications
Distributed in the United States and internationally by
CRCS Publications
(Write for current list of worldwide distributors.)
Cover Design: Image and lettering by Rebecca Wilson

CONTENTS

INTRODUCTION

*"I am a poet, a seeker and a confessor, obligated
to truth and sincerity. I have a mission, albeit
small and confined; to help other seekers understand and cope with the world, if only by
assuring them that they are not alone."*
                    ---HERMAN HESSE

Because I firmly believe that squares and oppositions are indicators of motivation, potential achievement and consciousness development, I have written
this book for people who struggle with contradictory
and seemingly mutually exclusive tendencies within
themselves, as indicated by the squares and oppositions of their natal astrology charts. Throughout the
chapters of this book, I am specifically addressing
the reader whose chart possesses a t-square configuration, a combination of planets, signs and houses
suggesting a pronounced strength or overemphasis, as
well as imbalance and deficiency. Since everyone experiences the t-square configuration upon numerous
occasions, because of the continually mobile influences of progressions and transits, the information
on the t-square presented here can be applied to any
person, whether or not he/she possesses a natal t-
square; it is also of particular relevance to any
person whose chart includes at least one square or
opposition.

This discussion of the t-square configuration is
basically a discussion of the conflicts and harmonies
suggested by the astrology chart, and the process of
constructively utilizing squares, oppositions, sextiles, trines and conjunctions, as well as developing
the qualities of the planets, signs, houses and aspects which may be weak or lacking.

Any planet or sign can be expressed constructively by including within its expression an awareness of opposite or conflicting planets and signs.
Oppositions can be synthesized and techniques for

resolving oppositions can be applied to squares and other aspects or planetary combinations. A stellium, a house or sign emphasis, or an emphasized element or mode may operate like a focal planet; a house or sign opposing a stellium, as well as a deficient element or mode may present problems similar to the problems of the empty space of the t-square. Techniques presented here for use with the t-square can therefore be applied to other variables in the chart.

In the last chapter of this book, *Becoming Whole*, I demonstrate some of the techniques of integration presented earlier - specifically, the technique of giving voice to one's planets as if they are personalities, and allowing them to dialogue with each other - this includes namecalling, arguing, cajoling - until some degree of cooperation is reached between at least a few planetary selves. The reader who wishes to experience the astrology map as a live map of psychological energies, before more abstractly attempting to understand its dynamics and potential, may wish to read *Becoming Whole* first.

This autobiographical chapter was not originally written for this book, but was written spontaneously during the month of my Saturn Return in 1979, when after completing the book, I experienced the power of my planets as live entities within myself. The process of giving life to them, and of allowing them to speak and dialogue, led to an internal transformation of energies which clearly altered the dynamics of my own t-square configuration, and precipitated a lengthy time period of substantial growth.

During the seven years since the original edition of this book *(How to Handle Your T-Square)* was published, I have been in training as a psychotherapist and clinical social worker, deepening my understanding of the human psyche and the process of psychological change. Although I still basically agree with the concepts presented here, my conceptualizations have, of course, evolved over time. For this reason, I choose to present a brief sketch of my current thinking in regard to the dilemmas posed by the t-square configuration.

The T-Square: Seven Years Later

In *The Symposium,* Plato describes how the gods originally created a perfectly whole, androgynous human being, one who was so self-complete that he/she lacked motivation, and defied the gods' orders to perform human tasks. As a result, the gods split this being into two selves - male and female - each one now motivated to find the missing half in order to experience completion.

This myth clearly explains the cause of the attraction between the sexes; it is also a fitting metaphor for the incompleteness known to the t-square person, who is forever driven to find the missing piece. Incomplete gestalts act like magnets; the incomplete person draws to herself, as well as attempts to create within herself, the missing part which will help to alleviate the agonizing sense of emptiness, of hanging open, of feeling exposed, or raw and amputated. A person with a t-square may also feel fragmented, as if she has been torn into many parts by forces beyond her control, as a result of some deepseated deficiency.

Squares and oppositions indicate splits within the personality which occur early in life. Failure to receive the right amount, kind and proportion of love/empathy and frustration (which, in appropriate doses, catalyzes growth), the evolving self is unable to retain its sense of unity, and to develop its capacity to integrate conflicting and often powerful drives; as a result, it splits into dissociated pieces. The t-square, in particular, suggests three splits, as well as a terrifying void. This void or empty space is usually related to some early trauma, which occurs at the time of the splitting, and which then leads to subsequent difficulties and deficiencies in this particular realm of life. Meanwhile, dissociated from each other, the three part-selves all develop their own specific behaviors and aims, without regard for each other, so that by adulthood, the person experiences his t-square as pulling in three different directions which seem incapable of coexisting. This pattern is often reinforced by the internalization of different and often clashing attitudes and actions from the parents and

environment. Similarly, a person with a grand cross configuration experiences internal splitting, but instead
of struggling with a three-way split, compulsive drive
and a void, he/she is pulled apart by four planetary
selves, and often feels paralyzed.

Because the t-square and grand cross indicate internal splitting, psychological and spiritual processes
oriented toward fusion of disparate parts or integration can help relieve some of the tension and suffering
which hinder wellbeing and effective action. In this
book, I focus upon what I now would call a *part*-ap-
proach to healing psychological splits - the use of
specific functions (such as indicated by the ruler of
the empty space or a trining planet) to ease the conflict and promote harmony. Such an approach is clearly
helpful. Yet from my vantage point now as a psychotherapist, I just as frequently utilize what could be considered the *whole*-approach to integration.

What is this *whole*-approach? Primarily, it involves discovering and creating pleasurable, loving,
unifying experiences within which all parts of ourselves can exist and within which our conflicts seem
literally to dissolve. Through such experiences, the
unifying warmth of Eros begins to heal the wounded
center, from where the splits originally occurred. The
deeper the wholeness at the center, the larger we become, and the more capable we are of guiding and integrating our many part-selves. As our center develops, we make choices about our lifespace which fulfill
our whole selves, rather than satisfy one part-self at
the expense of another. Psychotherapy, at its best,
involving a loving, trusting bond with the therapist,
helps to create a plethora of *whole*-experiences within which unification can occur.

It *is* possible to overcome the debilitating influences of squares and oppositions, and to experience the blessings of purposeful action and illuminated consciousness. But we must proceed slowly, step-
by-step, deepening our understanding while simultaneously learning to create more experiences within
our lives which help us to become whole.

8

WHAT IS A T-SQUARE?

Few characteristics of an astrological chart are as significant as the configurations made by planets in aspect to each other. Of the five major aspect configurations found most frequently in birthcharts (the stellium, t-square, grand cross, grand trine and yod), the t-square is the most common, and occurs in as many as 40 percent of all natal horoscopes. The t-square indicates not only the primary conflicts a person experiences, but also the talents and personal characteristics which he or she is motivated to develop, and which can lead to considerable achievement and satisfaction if expressed constructively.

What is a t-square? Do you have one in your natal chart? What does it mean? How can you best express it? If you don't have a t-square, what can you learn about the configuration that will enable you to make beneficial use of planetary energies, and to respond favorably to transits or progressions forming a t-square to a square or opposition in your chart? How can you deepen your understanding of the people in your life who possess t-square configurations? How can you help them to channel their energies effectively?

Definition

Technically, a t-square involves three or more planets. At least two of these planets are in opposition to each other, which means that they occur approximately 180 degrees apart, with an 8 degree orb allowable which establishes the range of the opposition at 172-180 degrees. One or both of these opposing planets may be conjunct (within 8 degrees of another planet.) Each, however, must also form a square to a planet which occurs approximately 90 degrees between them.

This planet which squares the opposition is known as the focal planet, and also has an allowable orb of 8 degrees, which means that it is positioned within the range of 82-98 degrees from each of the opposing planets. The focal planet, like either or both of the opposing planets, may also be part of a conjunction.

In most cases, the opposing planets and the focal planet which form a t-square are in the same mode by sign - cardinal (Aries, Cancer, Libra, Capricorn), fixed (Taurus, Leo, Scorpio, Aquarius), or mutable (Gemini, Virgo, Sagittarius, Pisces). The sign and the house opposing the focal planet are usually empty. If a planet opposes the focal planet, the configuration formed is not a t-square but a grand cross.

Example:

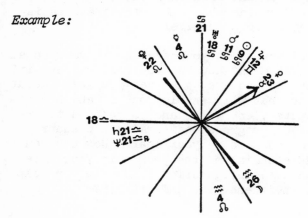

In this example, Pluto and the Moon are the opposing planets and Venus is the focal planet. Pluto and the Moon form an opposition with a four-degree orb. The square between Venus and Pluto has a one-degree orb, and the Venus/Moon square a three-degree orb. All three planets involved in this t-square o-cur in fixed signs. Venus, the focal planet, is positioned in Taurus in the eighth house, and no planets are in opposition to Venus,

10

*or are positioned in either Scorpio or the second
house. The degree opposite Venus, 23 Scorpio, is considered to be the empty space or empty degree of the
t-square. This is an example of a <u>strong</u> t-square
configuration.*

Variations and Strength

A t-square is particularly strong if it consists
of more than three planets, if all of its planets are
within a tight orb (less than three degrees), if it
contains one or more exact aspects (less than one degree), if it is angular, or if the focal planet is at
the midpoint of the two opposing planets. It is weak
if one planet is in a sign of a different mode than
the other two planets (i.e., Mars at 27 Pisces, Jupiter at 0 Cancer, Sun at 2 Capricorn), if orbs are over
six degrees, or if a planet occurs in the sign opposite
the focal planet and nearly squares or opposes one of
the planets in the t-square. A planet occurring in the
sign opposite the focal planet should be at least 15
degrees away from opposition; otherwise the configuration formed might qualify as a grand cross, or as a
combination t-square/grand cross.

The diagrams on the following pages illustrate a
number of possible t-square configurations. Most of
these variations have already been described above.
Note that if one planet in the configuration makes a
square or opposition with an eight to ten degree orb
to another planet, and all of the other aspects in the
configuration have orbs of less than eight degrees, a
weak t-square is formed. If an opposition squares the
ascendant/descendant axis, the midheaven/nadir axis or
the nodal axis, the configuration formed may express
itself alternately as a weak t-square and as a weak
grand cross.

General Meaning

A t-square is an imbalanced but dynamic configuration. The two squares, which both involve the focal

VARIATIONS OF THE T-SQUARE

Consider the degrees and signs below to be occupied by natal planets.

A *very strong* t-square. Orbs are nearly all exact.

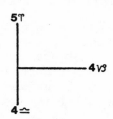

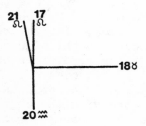

A *very strong* t-square. Orbs are close, and the conjunction gives added weight to the configuration.

A *very strong* t-square. Although the orb of the opposition is 6 degrees, the focal planet lies at the midpoint of the opposing planets.

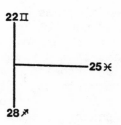

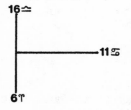

A *strong* t-square. Technically, the opposition is out of orb. However, the focal planet at the midpoint of the opposing planets strengthens the configuration.

A *strong* t-square. An
exact square and the
6 degree midpoint of
the Gemini planets
tighten the configur-
ation.

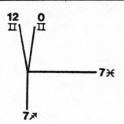

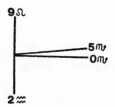

A *strong* t-square. Orbs
average about 3 degrees.

A *moderate* t-square. Orbs
average about 5 degrees.

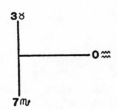

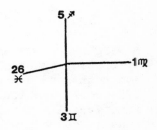

A *moderate* t-square. Orbs
are not close, but the
focal planet conjunction
gives added weight to the
configuration.

A *moderate* t-square.
A planet occurs in the
sign opposite the focal
planet, but is not even
within 20 degrees of
squaring or opposing any
planets in the t-square.

A *weak* t-square. A planet
occurs in the sign oppo-
site the focal planet,
and weakly squares a planet in the t-square. This
configuration is a combination weak t-square and
weak grand cross.

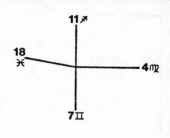

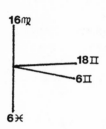

A *weak* t-square. Technically, most of the orbs
are too wide. However,
two of the squares are
nearly exact, and the
Gemini midpoint of 12 de-
grees is only one degree
orb from the Virgo/Pisces
midpoint of 11 degrees.

A *weak* t-square. The
focal planet is in a
mutable rather than a
cardinal sign.

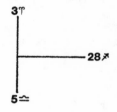

A *weak* t-square. The Leo/
Scorpio square is techni-
cally out of orb.

A *very weak* t-square. The
opposition squares the
ascendant and descendant.
This configuration would
function alternately as a
weak t-square and as a
weak grand cross.

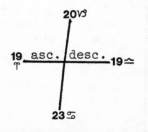

planet, create frustration and tension which interfere with the natural, constructive expression of the planet according to the sign and house in which it is positioned. This planet seems to be pulled in two directions by the opposition. Because the opposing planets and their signs and houses are unintegrated and out of balance, they are in conflict, and their conflict increases the pressure experienced at the focal planet. The attempts of the focal planet to cope with this pressure, to regain its balance and to express itself freely usually results in a powerful release of energy, (often expressed in a compulsive, wasteful or extreme manner) and a call to action.

The t-square demands action. Because it provides its own source of motivation, it indicates the potential for considerable achievement. The nature of this achievement is usually related to the nature of the focal planet, its sign and house, and the aspects which it forms within the natal chart.

A person with a t-square frequently wastes considerable energy overemphasizing the focal planet without giving due consideration to other sides of his or her personality. The sign and house opposite the focal planet, in the area frequently referred to as the empty space, indicate the gaps or deficiencies in his personal development - qualities and areas of life which, if developed, can enable him to express his focal planet in a moderate, balanced and constructive manner.

Sometimes, a person with a t-square escapes from the problems generated by the focal planet by overemphasizing the sign and house of the empty space. He or she leans too much in one direction, until problems here become overwhelming, then shifts gears completely and leans too heavily in the opposite direction, without much understanding of true meaning indicated by that sign and house. This tendency to swing compulsively from one extreme to another usually does not operate to his advantage, because the development of the empty space and the constructive expression of the focal planet are linked, and must be approached simultaneously.

Considerations

When interpreting the t-square, all of the following should be considered:

1) The mode or quadruplicity of the t-square. Is it cardinal, fixed or mutable? Are all of its planets in the same mode? The mode of the configuration describes how its energy is experienced and expressed. Cardinal t-squares are the most dynamic, active and crisis-oriented; fixed t-squares are the most powerful, determined and self-willed; mutable t-squares are the most restless, scattered and changeable.

2) The focal planet, its direct or retrograde motion, its placement by sign and house, and the house or houses it rules in the natal chart. (These houses will also experience the tension and motivation generated by the t-square.) The focal planet may be the most dominant planet in the chart, and the source of a large percentage of an individual's energy. *It must be used, and used wisely.* A secret of using the t-square effectively is to learn to express the focal planet in a positive manner, rather than be driven by its tension to compulsive activity, excess and overcompensation.

3) The opposing planets, their direct or retrograde motion, their placement by sign and house, and the houses which they rule in the natal chart. Each of these planets contributes to the expression of the focal planet, interfering with its functioning or spurring it to express itself in a more beneficial manner.

4) The nature of the opposition and the squares which form the t-square. How compatible are the planets involved in each aspect? How do they function together? How close, and therefore how strong is the aspect? The closest of these aspects indicates the greatest stress experienced by the t-square, as well as the means for alleviating that stress.

5) The empty space of the t-square - the degree, sign and house opposite the focal planet. If there are two focal planets in conjunction, the empty degree will be their far midpoint. The empty space needs to be consciously developed in a positive manner, so that the t-square individual does not need to overcompensate for his or her inadequacies by blindly throwing more undirected energy into the focal planet, and does not retreat from the tensions of the focal planet by reverting to the most negative manifestations of the empty space. The Sabian Symbol for the degree of the empty space is often a key to the quality which most needs to be developed.

6) The ruler of the sign of the empty space, and its position by sign and house in the natal chart. (e.g., If the sign of the empty space is Cancer, the ruler is the Moon.) This planet is frequently a key to *how* that sign may most easily be expressed. Since that sign is already expressed indirectly in the house of its ruler, its influence can be applied to other areas of the chart, particularly to the empty house. If the ruler is one of the planets of the t-square, then it particularly needs to be expressed constructively.

7) The trines and sextiles which occur in the natal chart between planets in the t-square and planets outside the t-square. These trines and sextiles can provide constructive channels of expression for the energy released by the t-square, or can serve as a means of escaping from the conflict. This is particularly true if a grand trine configuration connects with the t-square, in which case the connecting planet is not only a means of escape but also a means of utilizing the energy of the grand trine. Trines or sextiles to the focal planet are most important. The closest trine or sextile is likely to be an alchemical agent, providing a means for transmuting the unfocused energy of the t-square into creative, productive action.

8) Favorable minor aspects (such as the quintile, semi-sextile and novile) formed to planets in the t-

square and particularly to the focal planet. These minor aspects are significant channels only if nearly exact (less than one degree in orb) or if few trines or sextiles occur to t-square planets.

9) Any direct midpoint patterns formed to the planets in the t-square, particularly to the focal planet. (e.g., If the focal planet Mars is 16 Leo, Mercury is 8 Gemini and Saturn is 24 Libra, then Mars is the Mercury/Saturn midpoint, since it is positioned sixty-eight degrees after Mercury and sixty-eight degrees before Saturn.) If the focal planet is at the midpoint of two planets not involved in the t-square, learning to express these planets harmoniously together will help the focal planet to function more effectively.

10) A planet occurring at the midpoint of the squares involved in the t-square. (e.g., If focal Jupiter at 24 Libra squares Saturn at 22 Cancer, a planet equidistant from Jupiter and Saturn, at 8 Virgo or at 8 Pisces, would be positioned at the Jupiter/Saturn midpoint.) This planet can be an aid to harmoniously integrating the planets in square.

Of all of the above considerations, probably the most important are the mode or quadruplicity, the squares and oppositions which form the t-square, the nature of the focal planet and empty space, and the favorable aspects, particularly trines and sextiles, formed to the t-square. These deserve special attention, and should be considered at length.

Mode

People with cardinal t-squares are the most active of all t-square types, and the most inclined to plunge into crises situations related to their personal activities, home and family life, love relationships or professional commitments. Inclined to go after what they want (unless Aries occupies their empty space), they involve themselves totally in the problems of their existence, thriving upon excitement and chal-

18

lenge. Often Aries-like, unless the focal planet is in Libra, they need to cultivate the positive Libran qualities - balance, moderation, awareness of other people, perspective, and the ability to evaluate and compromise.

People with fixed t-squares display considerable strength of will, concentrated power and determination, particularly in regard to satisfying their own desires; they build up their energy slowly and then release it in a powerful manner, like a truck climbing a steep hill and then speeding down the other side. Goal-oriented and persevering, they stubbornly and forcefully adhere to their principles, refusing to compromise and resisting any attempts by other people to control their expression of energy. They can benefit by discovering constructive outlets for the energy generated by their frustrated desires, and by reformulating their value system in order to become more sensitive to other people's desires and needs.

People with mutable t-squares are usually over-adaptable, changeable, restless, versatile and very much concerned with and influenced by ideas and personal relationships. Their nervous mental energy and their suggestibility incline them to scatter their energies widely, dabbling in a multitude of diverse interests or flitting from one personal interaction to another. Because they adapt themselves so easily to their changing circumstances, they often seem vacillating and weak-willed. Like a team of water skiers in formation, these people need to cultivate balance in relationship to others, often by discovering a purpose or mission which centers them and keeps them from being pulled in too many directions.

Squares and Oppositions

Every t-square consists of at least two squares. These squares, like all squares, indicate internal tension resulting from two parts of oneself which clash, and which create a frustration that can only be resolved by action. This frustration is therefore a source of motivation, a drive to achieve or to express

19

oneself in a concrete, productive manner. However, the activities which one undertakes bring satisfaction only if they express the energies of both of the planets, signs and houses involved in the square.

When interpreting either a square or an opposition, the nature of the planets and their compatibility, the nature of the signs, and the exactness of the aspect all must be taken into consideration. An applying aspect is usually stronger than a separating aspect (particularly if it involves only outer planets) because it is likely, at some point in one's life, to become exact by progression.

Oppositions are generally more complex than squares. Since both planets in a t-square opposition exert their pressure upon the focal planet, the meaning of the opposition should be considered at length.

An opposition, like the t-square as a whole, denotes an imbalance. Two parts of oneself, indicated by the planets, signs and houses involved in the opposition, are not simply clashing; they are pulling oneself in two entirely different directions. The net result can be one or more of several different possibilities:

1) A person may feel torn apart and paralyzed because so much of his or her energy is involved in an internal tug-of-war. Because he equally accepts both parts of himself and does not know how to integrate them, he may be unable to make a decision and act.

2) He may fluctuate between expressing one part of himself and expressing the other part. One part may gain control for a minute, an hour, a day or even a year before the balance shifts and the other part takes over.

3) He may, because he is unable to accept one part of himself, project that part onto another person, viewing it as a quality of that other person rather than owning it as a dimension of his own being. This inability to experience both sides of himself may

result in feelings of alienation from other people. Because he is at odds with the people upon whom he has projected his unwanted qualities, he may experience frequent breaks or separations in his personal relationships.

4) He may actually choose to interact with people who express one side of his opposition (perhaps because it is a side of one of their oppositions). With them, he can overtly enact the battle that is actually taking place within his own psyche.

5) He may deny one side of himself completely, forcing it to operate in an unconscious or compulsive manner. This expression of the opposition is most likely to occur if one side of the opposition is stronger - because it is a planet in its own sign or house or located precisely on an angle, or because it is a conjunction or series of conjunctions. Denial does not rid of the unwanted characteristic, but rather strengthens it. As Carl Jung so aptly wrote, "You always become the thing you fight the most."

6) He may experience one part of himself as good and one part as bad, and strive continually to keep the expression of the bad part under control. This is particularly likely to happen if the opposition occurs between one of the relatively conscious or mental planets (Sun, Mercury, Jupiter or Saturn) and one of the relatively unconscious or emotional planets (Moon, Venus, Mars, Uranus, Neptune or Pluto). In this case, the conscious or mental planet is likely to voice its needs in terms of a "should" (e.g., Sun in Virgo in the tenth house: "You *should* work in the office several nights a week and finish your report."), and attempt to win control over the unconscious or emotional planet, which is experienced in terms of a nagging "want" (e.g., Moon in Pisces in the fourth house: "But I *want* to get home early enough to have a relaxing dinner with my family."). When a person satisfies the former at the expense of the latter, he may feel in control but his life may seem empty or meaningless; when he

satisfies the latter at the expense of the former, he may experience emotional satisfaction, but he is also likely to feel anxious and out of control.

If one polarity of the opposition is related by planet or sign to one's twelfth house, it is usually viewed negatively. For example, if a person's twelfth house contains Moon in Gemini, and either Cancer or Mercury is a part of the opposition, then the Cancer or Mercury polarity is not likely to be accepted easily, or to be allowed much conscious expression.

An opposition does not have to function in a detrimental manner. The position of its planets 180 degrees apart from each other can enable a person to expand his or her consciousness wide enough to tolerate the ambiguity and the tug of opposing forces; this expansion of consciousness can result in the objectivity and perspective necessary to create a meaningful compromise or synthesis between the two parts of his psyche and the two areas of his life. Once the parts of oneself that have been projected onto others are owned and accepted, relationships will become easier, more cooperative and less alienating.

Focal Planet

The focal planet of a t-square frequently operates like a dictator; it wants to predominate over all the other planets which make up the personality. The pressure exerted by the opposing planets which square it provide it with considerable energy; however, the frustration and stress which is at the source of this excess energy can lead the focal planet to break loose in an undisciplined, compulsive manner. Frequently, it seems to be out of control, acting apart from rather than in cooperation with the other planets in the chart.

The energy released by the focal planet can provide the motivation necessary to develop a talent or personal characteristic to the utmost, and to apply it in a practical and beneficial manner. This accomplishment can be expressed not only through the house in which the planet is positioned and the house or houses which it rules in the chart, but also in every area of life, particularly career and personal relationships. However, this talent or skill is often developed and expressed in an extreme manner, at the expense of other areas of the personality, particularly the area indicated by the empty space. Unless the focal planet is able to recognize and incorporate within itself the awareness of this empty sign and house, as well as the awareness of the needs of the other planets in the t-square and in the rest of the chart, it is not likely to bring full satisfaction.

A virtue, when carried to an extreme, usually becomes a vice. An overdevelopment of the Venusian qualities of love and devotion can result in the loss of oneself in another person; an overdevelopment of Saturnian responsibility and achievement can lead to emotional deprivation and depression; an overdevelopment of Neptunian inspiration and spirituality can lead to impracticality and chaos which prevent one from functioning effectively in the material world.

The strength of a focal planet, in relation to the other planets in a chart, depends upon a number of factors. It is likely to be especially strong, and probably the most dominant planet in a chart if it is one or more of the following: 1) in its own sign, 2) in its own house, 3) closely conjunct an angle, 4) stationary, or 5) the midpoint (within one degree) of the two planets in opposition. If the aspects within the t-square are nearly exact, if there are many aspects (at least five) to the focal planet, or if the focal planet is the midpoint of several planetary combinations in the chart, its influence is particularly intensified. Likewise, if there are two focal planets as a result of a conjunction, both of these planets are likely to dominate the chart. As in all conjunctions, they will express their energies together in a concentrated manner.

When interpreting a focal planet, its sign, its house, and the house or houses which it rules in the

23

natal chart must all be taken into consideration. The
sign indicates how the planet expresses its energies -
in an impulsive, excitable, quick and active manner if
in Aries, in an emotional, self-protective, nurturing
and perhaps clinging manner if in Cancer. The house
indicates the area of life which it most frequently
influences. The expression of the focal planet also
influences the house or houses which it rules in the
natal chart, particularly if that house is devoid of
planets. Frequently, when people are able to work out
the many problems they experience in the focal house
of the chart, they begin to experience considerable
stress in the house or houses ruled by the focal planet; they then must turn their attention to this area
of life until they resolve the problems manifested
there.

When a planet is retrograde natally, it indicates
energy that is turned inward, that is often not expressed outwardly until late in life (when and if that
planet turns direct by progression), and which may
manifest on a subconscious level, creating psychological or physical problems which are difficult to diag-
nose and overcome. (For more information on retrograde
planets, see Bil Tierney's *Perceptions in Astrology*
or the author's article, "Retrograde Planets in Detail," contained within her collection of articles
Turning Squares into Trines.) Usually, a retrograde
focal planet weakens the influence of a t-square because it does not fuel the motivation to release energy
through concrete action. The years during which a focal
planet is stationary by progression are frequently the
most significant years of a person's life, because of
the transformation which occurs in the expression of
this planet. The chapter on transits and progressions
later in this book will discuss this phenomenon in more
depth.

Occasionally, a situation occurs in a chart which
baffles the mind of the interpreter: the focal planet
is the ruler of the empty space. Mercury in Sagittarius,
for example, is the focal planet, and also the ruler of
the empty sign of Gemini. This situation is not as complex as it may first appear; it creates an additional

link between the focal planet and empty space, and indicates the importance of expressing the energy of the focal planet constructively, both in the focal sign and house, and in accordance with the sign and house of the empty space.

A focal planet can be expressed in an extremely negative or positive manner. The next chapter, which interprets each focal planet position, describes these negative and positive manifestations.

The Empty Space

The empty space of the t-square, particularly if no planets occupy its sign and house, indicates a deficiency or "hole" in the personality. Usually, a t-square person feels helpless and insecure when attempting to use energies indicated by the sign or when focusing upon the area of life indicated by the house of the empty space. With little understanding of this sign or house, he or she is stumped when trying to develop this quality or area of life. Frequently, interacting with people who have an emphasis of the sign or house in question can be an aid to understanding exactly what qualities are lacking and how they can be developed.

The empty space of the t-square is similar in many ways to the lack of an element. In both cases, a person may be aware of a personal deficiency or of an imbalanced lifestyle, and may overcompensate by striving too hard or too compulsively to express the energy and/or area of life in question. The striving itself is desirable. But without a complete understanding of this deficiency and of how the missing sign, house or element can be cultivated, and without an attempt to develop this facet of being in an integrated or balanced manner, the person usually fails to overcome his inadequacy. Escaping from the conflicts represented by the focal planet rather than trying actively to resolve them is especially likely to compound the problem.

The sign of the empty space indicates the qualities which need to be developed; the house indicates the area of life through which they need to be expressed. If the sign of the empty space is intercepted, or if its ruler is retrograde or positioned in the twelfth house, a person will experience particular difficulty in understanding the meaning of the empty sign and expressing it overtly. The ruler of this sign does indicate how, and in what area of life, these qualities are already being expressed. By developing the planetary function of the ruler, and understanding the process by which it operates according to its sign and house in the natal chart, a person can often learn to apply its influence to other areas of life, and particularly to the area indicated by the empty space.

The Sabian Symbol for the degree of the empty space, which is in the same degree but the opposite sign of the focal planet, often provides a key to the facet of the personality which needs to be developed. (Note that when using the Sabian Symbols, 16 degrees 0 minutes is considered to be 16 degrees, but 16 degrees 1 minute is 17 degrees.) In the case of a focal planet conjunction, this empty degree is the degree opposite the midpoint of the conjunction, although the degrees opposite each of the focal planets should also be considered. For more information on the Sabian Symbols, see *An Astrological Mandala* by Dane Rudhyar. The use of Sabian Symbols, as well as other techniques for working with the t-square, will be discussed at more length in a later chapter entitled, "How to Handle Your T-Square."

The empty space of the t-square cannot be developed effectively without using the focal planet. One of the ways of mastering the t-square is to learn to express the focal planet in a constructive manner, in accordance with the sign and house of the empty space.

Dynamics of the T-Square

A complete understanding of the aspects made to the t-square by planets outside the configuration is impossible without first understanding the precise dynamics which occur among all of the variables of the t-square discussed in the preceding pages - the squares, the opposition, the focal planet and the empty space. The energy of the t-square seems to operate in two directions: 1) from the opposing planets, through the squares, to the empty space, and 2) from the focal planet, through the squares, to the opposition.

In the first instance, a person experiences considerable tension because he feels pulled in two directions by the opposing planets, or struggles with difficulties in his personal relationships. In a state of paralysis, the only way he knows how to free his energy is to release his tension through the focal planet, acting forcefully according to its sign and house. Because his behavior here is usually extreme and creates havoc in this dimension of his life, he attempts to escape from this new conflict by fleeing into the sign and house of the empty space. In this case, he is neither resolving the opposition nor effectively harnessing the energy of the focal planet; nor is he likely to be constructively developing his empty sign and house. He will not be able to make any headway with the dilemmas of his t-square until he stops running away from each problem that surfaces, and decides instead to regain center, to confront each problem, and to translate the tension he experiences into constructive action. This dynamic is usually the most powerful of the two dynamics if there are several oppositions, or if the opposition is the most exact aspect in the t-square.

In the second instance, a person expresses his focal planet in an extreme and/or compulsive manner, generating conflict in accordance with the nature of the planet, its sign and its house. This extremism creates an imbalanced state of affairs which aggravates the imbalance denoted by the opposing planets. The opposition then becomes the primary conflict, expressing itself in a seesawing manner, in terms of projection or denial of one of its energies, in terms of paralysis, or in terms of separation or alienation in relationships. Eventually, the dilemma of the opposition may lead the person to step back from his life, regain center, and develop the awareness necessary to synthesize the two opposing parts of himself. When the opposition is resolved, the focal planet can be expressed in a more controlled, balanced and constructive manner. This dynamic of the square is likely to predominate if the squares are closer in orb than the opposition, if there are two or more focal planets, or if the focal planet is particularly powerful by virtue of being in its own sign or house, on an angle, or stationary.

Favorable Aspects

Perhaps the most helpful aids to integrating and expressing the t-square productively are the trines, sextiles and other favorable aspects between planets involved in the t-square and other planets on the chart. Several situations are possible.

Consider the following example:

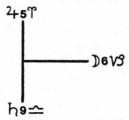

In this example, and in any t-square:

1) A planet may <u>trine</u> the focal planet, and perhaps semi-sextile one of the planets of the opposition while inconjuncting the other planet. In the above example, an aspecting planet could be positioned near 6 degrees Taurus or 8 degrees Virgo.

2) A planet may <u>sextile</u> the focal planet, and perhaps semi-sextile one of the planets of the opposition while inconjuncting the other planet. In the above example, the aspecting planet could be positioned near 8 degrees Scorpio or 6 degrees Pisces.

3) A planet may trine one of the opposing planets, frequently also sextiling the other planet (or vice versa) and inconjuncting the focal planet. In the above example, the aspecting planet could be positioned near 6 degrees Gemini or 6 degrees Leo.

4) A planet may trine one of the opposing planets, frequently sextiling the other planet (or vice versa), and semi-sextiling the focal planet. In the above example, the aspecting planet could be positioned near 6 degrees Sagittarius or 6 degrees Aquarius.

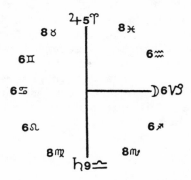

In some cases, an aspecting planet will trine or sextile one of the planets in a t-square without aspecting any of the others. This could easily occur because trines have larger orbs than sextiles or inconjuncts, which in turn have larger orbs than semi-sextiles; it could also occur because the aspecting planet may be significantly higher or lower by degree than all but the planet in the t-square which it aspects. In the above example, a planet at 14 Aquarius would trine Saturn, but would neither sextile Jupiter nor semi-sextile the Moon; it is not only considerably higher by degree than Jupiter and the Moon, but it is also out of range of the orbs commonly used for the semi-sextile (2 degrees) and for the sextile (4 degrees).

A planet that trines or sextiles one of the planets in the t-square but does not aspect the others can be an aid in channelling the energy of the t-square, but it will not be nearly as important as a planet

29

which aspects all three t-square planets. Certainly, aspects to the focal planet, particularly trines, should be considered the most powerful. The importance of an aspecting planet will depend not only upon the number of aspects which it makes to the t-square, and whether or not it aspects the focal planet, but also upon the nature of the aspect it makes (trines are strongest, followed by both sextiles and inconjuncts, and lastly by semi-sextiles), and the exactitude of its orbs.

A trine (120 degrees, 6-8 degree orb) indicates an easy flow of energy from one planet to another, with both planets able to express themselves in a natural harmonious and often habitual manner. A trine to a t-square planet may serve as an escape from the problems of the t-square, but it may also provide a constructive outlet for some of the frustration generated within the t-square. The outlet can be determined by interpreting the aspecting planet in question in terms of its nature, its sign and its house, as well as the aspect it makes to the t-square and how it functions in relation to the t-square planet.

A sextile (60 degrees, 4 degree orb) indicates a more creative and mental outlet than does the trine, but requires a little more effort. The squares within the t-square can provide the necessary motivation.

A semi-sextile (30 degrees, 2 degree orb) functions like a weak sextile and requires even a greater expenditure of energy. It is often more difficult to express because it usually occurs between signs which are not easily integrated.

An inconjunct (150 degrees, 4 degree orb) is the least harmonious of these four aspects. Indicating energies which are out of gear and lead to subconscious tension (manifesting as hard-to-diagnose physical or psychological problems, or more beneficially, as artistic skills), the inconjunct does not easily express itself in the overt, active manner required by the t-square. As a result, an aspecting planet which trines the focal planet may provide the most effective outlet for the t-square, but the inconjunct which may form to an opposing planet generates problems of its own which must be confronted.

Of the four aspect patterns described earlier, probably the easiest is #4 - a planet trining an opposing planet, sextiling the other opposing planet, and semi-sextiling the focal planet. This planet is powerful only if the semi-sextile is well within its 2 degree orb and can be utilized by the individual.

Apart from the above-mentioned aspects, three other minor aspects deserve special mention: the quintile, the semi-square and the sesquiquadrate. A quintile (72 degrees, 2 degree orb) formed to a t-square planet is significant if the t-square makes few (or only weak) trines or sextiles. The quintile indicates the ability to synthesize diverse energies in a highly unique and creative way, often through tapping levels of consciousness which are not easily accessible. Although difficult to understand and express, a quintile is most likely to be activated if it occurs to a focal planet with no trines or sextiles; the resulting tension in such a t-square will often force an individual into a state of consciousness which is stressful, but which also expands awareness, reveals hidden talents and stimulates creative self-expression.

The semi-square (45 degrees, 2 degree orb) and the sesquiquadrate (135 degrees, 2 degree orb) are not normally considered favorable aspects. The former indicates an active tension, similar to but weaker than the square, and less conscious; it is both a source of conflict and motivation. The latter also indicates conflict, but particularly the conflict or tension which results *from* action rather than that which leads *to* action; the sesquiquadrate, like the inconjunct, is a step between the ease of the trine and the divided but awakened consciousness of the opposition.

A planet may occur within the t-square, semi-squaring the focal planet and an opposing planet and forming a sesquiquadrate to the other opposing planet. Or, it may occur outside the t-square, semi-squaring an opposing planet and forming a sesquiquadrate to the focal planet and the other opposing planet. Although a planet in either of these positions increases the stress experienced within the t-square, it also provides another dynamic outlet for the release of energy. Natal (and transiting) planets located at any of these points can be a potent source of transformation. Frequently, they introduce new opportunities into one's life which enable one to harness the energies and resolve many of the problems denoted by the t-square.

Combined Configurations

Occasionally, the chart of a t-square person will contain another aspect configuration,* one which shares a planet in common with the t-square. Two inconjuncts which form a yod (also called the finger of God) to a planet in the t-square create an important dual configuration. If the focal planet of the yod is also the focal planet of the t-square, the empty space of the yod (the degree between the two planets in sextile) occurs in the same area as the empty space of the t-square. It will respond, as the t-square does, to transiting planets which enter its sphere of influence. Since the yod usually brings about transformative experiences which result in a sense of mission, the combination t-square/yod, when triggered, can lead to purposeful and creative achievement, expressed in accordance with the nature of the focal planet or planets of both configurations.

A combination grand trine/t-square is likewise a dynamic configuration, but it can too easily influence a person to escape into the grand trine, losing himself in habitual patterns of frenetic activity (grand fire trine), compulsive work or moneymaking (grand earth trine), ceaseless intellectualizing (grand air trine) or excessive but undisclosed emotionalism(grand

---

Readers unfamiliar with the stellium, grand trine or yod should consult the appendix, which contains material on these configurations originally published in the author's ART OF CHART INTERPRETATION.

water trine). In its most positive expression, a grand trine can lend its practical, active, intellectual and interactive, or emotional ease to the t-square, enabling the t-square individual to draw upon these energies as he struggles with the problems of his t-square and learns to apply himself productively.

A combination t-square/stellium is also a powerful combination, but can be the most difficult of any combined aspect configuration because the expression of a number of planets must be integrated with the t-square opposition. A stellium at one of the opposing planets is likely to exert a dominant and usually oppressive influence over the planet it opposes. A stellium at the focal planet usually results in a large number of squares which must be integrated and expressed in an active, overt manner. This stellium/t-square combination generates a powerhouse of energy and can result in severe tension which totally undermines an individual's functioning, or can be channelled into extremely self-motivated and effective action. The underdevelopment of the empty space is particularly an issue here, because the focal planets, signs and houses are overemphasized to an extraordinary degree.

Positive/Negative Expression

The t-square configuration, at its worst, can indicate serious psychological problems. It can suggest a tendency to develop one side of one's personality at the expense of all other sides. It can denote a neurosis or complex, perhaps in the form of an obsession, which dominates the person to the extent that he or she feels possessed, enslaved, or out of control. The amount of tension generated by the t-square can create a situation of frenetic upheaval, a nervous disorder which results in a constant state of anxiety and crisis. The nature of the disorder is usually indicated by the position of the focal planet, although its problems may be disguised by the problems which arise in the area of the empty sign and house.

On the other hand, the energy released by the t-square is also the source of its strength and its po-

tential for achievement. The overdevelopment of one
side of the personality can indicate a clear sense of
direction or focus, an ability to specialize and develop remarkable skills or qualities related in meaning to the focal planet's position. The tension can be
a source of motivation and drive, enabling a person
to develop himself to the fullest extent; it can even
provide the motivation necessary to express the t-
square in a more balanced and integrated manner.

The t-square is the most common configuration in
the charts of successful people. The focal planet is
usually an indicator of their talents and accomplishments. The more exact the t-square, and the more extreme its functioning, the more likely a person is to
experience both its severe psychological stress and its
potential for achievement.

Each person with a natal t-square must decide for
himself: Is it more important to fulfill the goal of
the focal planet and experience the satisfaction that
such accomplishment brings, although possibly at the
expense of one's health, relationships, or peace of
mind? Or is it wiser to aim for balance and moderation
rather than greatness, to focus less upon developing
the potential of the focal planet and more upon overcoming personal deficiencies and developing one's
capacity to live a fully integrated and well-rounded
life?

Perhaps both are possible, and a person who is
driven compulsively to release his tensions in one
area of life experiences less satisfaction and achieves
less of significance than a fully integrated person who
is also active, productive and highly directed.

FOCAL PLANETS

Although the following interpretations are concerned with the positive and negative expressions of
focal planets, they can help you understand how you
might or might not express the other planets in your
t-square and any other planets in your chart. Understanding the positive manifestation of the planet
which rules your empty sign can especially help you to
express the energies of that planet beneficially, and
to apply its influence to the area of your life denoted by the empty space.

The positive and negative interpretations included in this chapter are extreme interpretations.
Few people will express any of their planets in such
a black and white manner. You are likely to discover
that you exhibit some of the destructive qualities of
your focal planet and your other strongly positioned
planets, and that you are gradually beginning to tune
in to their more constructive qualities.

Because these interpretations do not include any
reference to signs or houses, you must modify each interpretation to take into account the sign or house
position of the planet in question. Your focal Venus,
for example, may influence your love relationships
and/or your attitudes toward money and possessions;
its placement in Taurus or Libra, or in the second or
seventh house, would indicate which of these meanings
is likely to predominate. However, if your Venus is
in Pisces in the ninth house, you must modify the interpretations given for Venus to take into consideration the influence of Pisces upon your ninth house
areas of life. Remember, however, that because a focal
planet is so powerful, its influence may extend over

all the houses, influencing above all your work and
your relationships.

You are likely to express a planet negatively if
that planet is heavily afflicted and if you make no
conscious attempt to understand and cultivate its positive expression. The negative expression of a planet
may result from allowing it to function in a compulsive, unconscious or extreme manner, or from failing
to incorporate into its expression an awareness of
other parts of yourself.

Your ability to express the positive dimensions
of a planet will depend upon the balance and integration you achieve between the many parts of yourself.
You can begin to develop such balance and integration
by cultivating self-awareness and perspective, by consciously paying attention to how you use your energy,
and by attempting at all times to act in a constructive manner, in accordance with your highest principles and ideals. In order to live a balanced life, you
must desire, above all, to bring all parts of yourself
into harmony rather than to experience the transient
pleasures that characterize a life of extremes.

The positive expression of a planet includes within it an awareness of its opposite. For example, an
effective and ultimately constructive demonstration of
your anger (Mars) is not likely to be an explosion of
temper in which you run roughshod over the feelings of
a loved one and threaten the bonds of trust within
your relationship; it is more likely to be a firm and
centered assertion of your feelings, which also takes
into consideration the other person's point of view
and your desire to maintain a relationship which is
mutually fulfilling (Venus). This Mars/Venus polarity
is one of five commonly accepted planetary polarities,
which include Sun/Moon, Moon/Saturn, Mercury/Jupiter,
and Jupiter/Saturn. Since the ten planets cannot be
clearly divided into five mutually exclusive sets of
polarities, the opposite expression of a planet may
not be one other planet, but rather a combination of
planetary influences. Frequently, however, useful polarities can be determined by considering the rulers

36

of opposite signs (e.g., Mercury and Jupiter, ruling
Gemini and Sagittarius) or of adjacent signs (e.g.,
Sun and Moon, ruling Cancer and Leo).

If the focal planet or another planet in your
chart is retrograde, it will usually operate in an
introverted or unconscious manner; the more overt expression of that planet will probably not manifest until that planet turns direct by progression. A later
chapter in this book, on the influence of transits
and progressions upon the t-square, considers this
phenomenon in more detail.

SUN

*"The will is essentially the activity
of the self which stands above the multiplicity...of drives, urges, desires
and wishes. The will is like the conductor of an orchestra."*
                              ROBERT ASSAGIOLI

*"You never kill the ego. You only find
that it lives in a larger house than
you thought."*   STANLEY KELEMAN

Negative Expression

If the Sun is the focal planet of your t-square,
you are likely to experience ego problems which stem
from a conflicted relationship with your father. Because you are unsure of your own identity and insecure
about your self-expression, you need to prove your importance to yourself and others. However, your feelings
of helplessness, powerlessness and insignificance may
lead you to assert your self-sufficiency, power and
significance all too loudly.

As a self-proclaimed celebrity, you may feel uncomfortable in social situations unless you are the
center of attention, impressing other people and win-
ning their approval. In your relationships, you may

boost your ego by making sure that you are in a position of control, able to dominate and make frequent
demands upon the other person. Whatever you do, you
tend to express yourself in a grand and often osten-
tatious manner, so that you will be seen and acknowledged and your creative accomplishments will win you
considerable attention.

Although you are proud, egocentric and inclined
to behave like a king and treat other people as your
subjects, your sense of identity remains shaky. When
you have no audience, when you are not number one, you
don't know who you are. The stress that you experience
in attempting to assert yourself and gain the appreciation of others may interfere with your health, resulting in disorders of the heart, spleen or upper
spine.

Positive Expression

When you tap into the positive energies of your
focal Sun, you will develop a firm and grounded awareness of your own identity. Your self-confidence will
spring not from the role you play or the response of
your audience, but from the contact you make with your
own center of gravity.

You will be centered, in touch with the Self behind the ego, the universal will which encompasses the
personal will. As a result, you will be able to identify with other people, to express yourself and to
assert yourself without imposing upon them. You will
make a creative contribution to society which not only
boosts your own self esteem, but which also enriches
other people's lives. Self-expressive and creative,
you will also be able to encourage other people's self-
expression and creativity. You will enjoy center stage,
but will also be capable of being a warm and appreciative audience.

Because you will be able to draw from your own
internal sources of energy, at your solar plexus and
in your heart, your vitality will be high and you will

38

radiate warmth and genuine affection. You will be proud, but your pride will be tempered with humility because you will know that the light which shines in you is not solely your own, but a mere flicker of a greater light which can shine through everyone.

Vocationally, you will be likely to function successfully in a management or executive position, or to find fulfillment in an occupation concerned with children, entertainment or the creative arts. A born leader, you will effectively take charge of others because you will be aware of the abuses of power, and will be sensitive to other people's ego needs as well as your own. You will be able to guide without controlling because you will be in control of yourself, able to conduct your own planetary orchestra and delight both yourself and others with its buoyant, expressive music.

MOON

"The personal life, deeply lived, takes you beyond the personal."
                    ANAIS NIN

"The nourishing person handles his unfulfilled needs himself rather than burdening others with them."
                    DR. JERRY GREENWALD

"The only way to hold is to let go."
                    MELISSA LEIFER

Negative Expression

If the Moon is the focal planet of your t-square, you experience emotional problems which stem from an early conflict with your mother, and which lead you to cling to some external form of security - your relationships with women, your family, or your home. You may form highly dependent relationships with people who are willing to play the maternal role and take care of you, or you may instead become a "supermom" yourself, so eager to be wanted that you overly respond to other people's needs and become smothering and over-protective. Whether you are male or female, your relationships with women are a considerable source of conflict to you, not only because you place so much importance upon them, but also because you look to women to fill the emotional vacuum you experienced with your own mother.

You are highly emotional, frequently at the mercy of your ever-changing moods, which may at times dominate your consciousness and leave you feeling weak and passive. Oversensitive to other people's reactions to you, you tend to take the most innocent remarks and gestures personally, feeling hurt and rejected when you do not get the response you so deeply desire, and withdrawing into a shell from which no one can pry you. So many of your problems stem from your inability to give up infantile hungers for the safety of the womb and the protection of a relationship or family life which guarantees unconditional love and complete protection from the insecurities of the outside world. Behavior patterns originating in childhood, old habits, and painful memories which seem to have a life of their own threaten your sense of freedom and your ability to function as a responsible, rational adult.

Your emotional insecurity may result in digestive disorders, or disorders of the lymph glands. If you are a woman, you may experience problems with your uterus or your breasts.

Positive Expression

When you have tapped into the positive expression of your focal Moon, you will have begun to develop the objectivity necessary to understand your early conditioning; you will be able to draw from your immense reservoir of emotional energy the motivation necessary to change behavior patterns which are no longer functional. Your relationships to women, your family life and your home will still be high priorities, but you will no longer look to them to satisfy all your emotional needs or to provide the security that only you yourself can provide. Indeed, you will have learned to respect and nurture the child within you, nourishing yourself in ways that your parents may not have been able to nourish you. Rather than deny or pamper the needs of your unhappy inner child, you will treat it tenderly but firmly, enabling it to grow into a healthy, emotionally fulfilled adult.

Your ability to deal with your emotions will enable you to respond sensitively to the feelings of other people, empathizing with their problems but also encouraging their self-sufficiency and not allowing them to become overly dependent upon you. Able to draw from the fertile grounds of your own subconscious and to establish an inner refuge within yourself, you will deeply appreciate the people in your life who in times of great need are willing to take care of you, but you will not allow yourself to cling to them or to revert to childish behavior so that they will rescue you from yourself.

Because you will be adept at handling emotional and domestic issues, you will be likely to find satisfaction in such nurturing occupations as counselling, daycare, nursing or homemaking, or in real estate, farming or restaurant work. Whatever occupation you choose, you will be able to relate on a sensitive, personal level with the public, responsive to their needs and capable of both giving and receiving emotional nourishment.

MERCURY

"The mind is its own place, and in it-self/Can make a Heaven of Hell, a Hell of Heaven."   JOHN MILTON

"Real knowledge comes not from intellect but from immediate contact...Knowledge depends on being."
    GURDJIEFF

Negative Expression

If Mercury is the focal planet in your t-square, you are likely to scatter your energies widely by dabbling in too many areas of interest or interacting with too many people. Overreacting to the stimulation of your environment, you are restless, flittering here and there in a frantic attempt to discharge your nervous energy. Frequently, you become lost in petty issues or concerns, losing all sense of perspective in your obsession with details. You may waste many hours in pointless conversation, chattering incessantly about the minor matters of your daily life and often focusing unduly upon your worries, anxieties and health problems. Your health, indeed, may be a source of stress, for you may suffer from nervous disorders, respiratory problems or ailments which interfere with the mobility of your shoulders and arms.

Your mind is hungry for knowledge, but you tend to be a collector of trivia because your approach to learning is superficial and disorganized; you absorb bits and pieces of factual data randomly, without concern for their meaning or implications, and with little desire to think for yourself and formulate your own answers. You intellectualize, rationalize, criticize and analyze constantly, unable to turn off the chatter of your thoughts and enjoy internal silence, to experience your feelings, or to listen quietly to another person. Your perfectionism, combined with your inclination to become carried away with words and thoughts, often results in your giving constant negative messages to yourself and others.

You may feel disconnected in your personal relationships because you are unable to connect with yourself or other people on non-verbal levels or to fully experience and accept another person. Often, you seek to establish connections by being of help to others, but because you have difficulty connecting on an equal level, you express yourself in an ingratiating or servile manner.

Positive Expression

Once you have mastered your focal Mercury, you
will be able to efficiently cope with and appreciate
the many details of your daily life without becoming
mired in them; you will develop a sense of perspective,
an awareness of priorities, and a purpose in your existence which enables you to perceive everything in
its proper place. Your ability to interact with diverse people, your wide range of practical skills and
your breadth of knowledge will contribute to a versa-
tility that is not lacking in depth, for you will
possess the mental discipline necessary to focus upon
one thing at a time and develop proficiency before
moving onto the next.

Aware of your abundance of nervous energy, you
will be inclined to meditate or rest frequently, so
that you can clear your mind of its accumulated poi-
sons, tune into the reality beneath your words and
thoughts, and listen quietly to other people. Physical
activity, an understanding of your mind/body relationship, a willingness to care for your health, and a
receptivity to your feelings and the feelings of others
will bring clarity and depth to your mental functioning. Able to flow with your experience, and able to
accept yourself and others rather than become a slave
to perfectionistic standards, you will be able to make
full contact in your daily interactions. You will not
need to scatter yourself too widely in a frantic attempt to connect with more and more people because the
quality of your connections will be deep and satisfying. You will be helpful to others and offer your services, without being overly obliging or allowing yourself to be used.

Your conscious attention to your mental processes
will enable you to pluck out the negative messages you
give yourself, and will enable your mind and body to
function in a healthy, constructive manner. With your
mind relaxed, clear and positive, you will be alert
and observant, picking up relevant stimuli in your
environment and organizing your reality in a meaningful way. Not only will you excel in common sense and

the ability to organize details, but you will be able
to frequently demonstrate your problem-solving skills,
your manual dexterity, and your efficiency in attending to daily tasks.

Because your positively functioning Mercury will
enhance your speaking and writing abilities and your
desire to exercise and improve your verbal skills, you
will be a fluent and accomplished speaker and/or writer. You may find considerable satisfaction working
in a communication-related occupation as an editor,
writer, teacher, reporter, librarian, typist, recep-
tionist or printer. Or, because of your desire to be
of service to other people and your concern with
healthy mind/body functioning, you may choose to work
in a health profession.

VENUS

*"Learning to love...is a high induce-
ment to the individual to ripen, to become something in himself...for what
would a union be of (persons) unclari-
fied and unfinished?"*
                    RAINER MARIA RILKE

*"In order to seek values, man must con-
sider himself worthy of enjoying them."*
                    NATHANIEL BRANDEN

*"The difficulty of love is that so many
people take you at your own evaluation."*
                    ANONYMOUS

*"Where you do not find love, put love,
and there you will find it."* ST. JOHN

Negative Expression

With Venus as the focal planet of your t-square,
you focus unduly on your personal relationships and
the love you do or do not receive from other people.

You would rather enter into or remain in an unfulfilling relationship than be alone, and you may even flit
from partner to partner in search of someone who can
give you the love you cannot give yourself. But because you cannot fully appreciate your own worth, or
because you are much more concerned with being loved
than with cultivating your own genuine feelings of
love for others, you usually form imbalanced and unsatisfying relationships with people you do not value
or who do not value you. After all, how can you care
about someone who is blind enough to care about you,
when you believe that all you deserve are people who
recognize your unworthiness, are incapable of loving
you, and leave you feeling all the more insatiable?

Your Venus gives you the ability to appear loving,
unselfish and devoted, but your appearance is usually
a phony one, masking only your fear of aloneness and
your eagerness to win the affection of others. Capable
of being whatever other people want you to be, you
usually try too hard to attract love by always being
charming, agreeable and accommodating, and by avoiding,
at any cost, disagreements and confrontations. "Peace
at any price," is your motto, and you are willing to
pay the price of a superficial relationship rather
than threaten your illusion of the harmony you experience with others.

Unable to find complete satisfaction in your relationships, you are likely to experience bouts of
pleasure-seeking, during which you indulge yourself
in material possessions, food, or a variety of sensual
pleasures. Greedily pampering yourself, you passively
expect all the good things of life to come to you, and
shy away from making an effort to go after what you
value or to become worthy of attracting people, possessions, and pleasurable experiences which you can
fully appreciate. Your indulgent approach to life may
weaken you physically, making you susceptible to disorders of the throat, glands or female sexual organs.

You tend to be vain, superficial and overly concerned with physical appearance and surface behavior.
Although you are interested in the arts, your lazy and

45

self-indulgent tendencies may keep you from developing artistic interests and abilities.

Positive Expression

When you learn to express your Venus construc- tively, you will be less inclined to look outward for love because you will love yourself. Able to experi- ence your own inner beauty and to enjoy the pleasures of your own company, you will be able to enrich your personal relationships and please others by simply being yourself rather than being a reflection of their needs and desires. Because you will be in possession of yourself, you will be able to encounter other people on a full and equal basis. The affection and love which you express will be genuine because you will be able to experience the beauty of another human being and because your primary motive will not be receiving love but rather giving from your own inner fullness.

Relationships will be of considerable importance to you, but will not be your only source of satisfac- tion because you will have learned to live a balanced life which includes the pleasures of work, people, solitude and leisure activities. Aware of your values in terms of relationships, you will be selective about forming friendships and partnerships. Because you will not be hungry for human contact or in need of being appreciated by everyone you meet, you will avoid form- ing unsatisfying or destructive relationships with people you do not value or who do not value you.

Your focal Venus will contribute to your ability to remain aware of other people's needs, to express yourself tactfully, to cooperate easily, and to main- tain smooth and comfortable interactions. The peace of mind you experience with yourself and the ease which you experience with others will not be a sur- face harmony which denies the reality of human con- flict, for you will be able to assert yourself when necessary, and to confront another person in a diplo- matic and sensitive manner. Your sensitivity to and interest in other people will be an aid to you pro- fessionally as well as personally, and may incline you to develop skills in counselling or public relations work.

Although your Venus will often function as a magnet, drawing to you the people and experiences that can meet your needs, you will not passively wait for life to come to you. You will cultivate your artistic interests and express yourself creatively, whether for your own personal satisfaction or for professional rewards. Not only will you appreciate the beauty of the world around you, but you will also exert an effort to contribute to that beauty yourself – perhaps by cultivating your personal appearance, gardening, caring for houseplants or decorating. If you are not interested in public relations, consulting or an artistic profession, you may select work related to nature, clothes, jewelry, or interior decorating.

Your positively functioning Venus will also enable you to appreciate sensual pleasures and material possessions without indulging yourself in spending sprees, eating binges or demeaning sexual encounters in order to experience satisfaction. You will develop your own earning power and manage your material resources in accordance with a value system which does not value money for its own sake, but rather for the quality of experience it can bring to your life. Able to appreciate what you have, you will not be at the mercy of a hunger for more possessions; in possession of yourself, you will be able to appreciate people and material goods without necessarily possessing them.

MARS

"Keep asking 'What do I desire?' The other important questions will follow."
        SAM KEEN

"You must learn to make every act count, since you are going to be here...too short a while for witnessing the marvels of it....The secret of doing is knowing when to not-do."
        CARLOS CASTANEDA

Negative Expression

If Mars is the focal planet of your t-square, you are overly concerned with satisfying your own desires. Unaware of and often oblivious to other people's feelings, desires or points of view, you want your own way, and are willing to provoke conflict in order to get it. In relationships, you are often impulsive and pushy, inclined to coerce the other person to conform to your wishes; at your worst, you may be cruel and even violent. Because you take offense easily and enjoy the stimulation of an argument or fight, you are frequently aggressive and belligerent in your dealings with people, and may be unwilling or unable to reveal your soft side or to enter into a warm and affectionate relationship.

Your difficulty in coping with the frustration of your desires means that you are usually seeking their immediate satisfaction. Sex is likely to be of considerable importance to you because it enables you to release your energy and experience the excitement which you crave; however, your tendency to focus upon your own satisfaction may incline you to be an insensitive sexual partner, and your undue emphasis upon the sexual and physical side of life may create anxiety which interferes with your sexual functioning.

Mars as the focal planet of your t-square also indicates that you lead a hyperactive and sometimes frenetic existence. Because you thrive on action, you frequently plunge into new activities with little forethought; your lack of direction and your inclination to begin a new project before you finish a previous one often leads you to scatter yourself too widely, wasting energy that could be expressed in a more productive manner. Your tendency to follow each impulse and act without restraint or self-control may lead to reckless behavior and accidents, as well as frequent arguments and confrontations with other people.

Your undisciplined lifestyle may also affect your physical functioning, resulting in burns, inflammations, fever or excessive bleeding. It may also lead to problems with elimination or to disorders of the arteries, muscular system, adrenal glands or male sex organs.

Positive Expression

Once you have learned to express your Martian energy constructively, you will be aware of your values and priorities, and will act in order to satisfy your deepest desires rather than allow yourself to become a slave to flitting impulses. Energetic, self-motivated, enthusiastic and active, you will immerse yourself fully in activities which are in keeping with your central purpose. You will think before plunging into some new adventure which could have disastrous consequences, for you will be able to bear the tension which results from delaying immediate satisfaction, channelling that frustrated energy into healthy physical activity.

Because you will be less inclined to begin every new project which appeals to you, because you will have cultivated patience and an awareness of timing, and because you will know the full satisfaction and release of energy which results from completing a project which requires more than a momentary expenditure of energy, you will be able to finish most projects you begin. Your awareness of your needs for immediate satisfaction will, at the same time, keep you from committing yourself to many activities which demand sustained work over a long period of time; you will be able to incorporate into your life activities of both short-term and long-term duration. Your life will remain exciting even when you have learned to moderate and control your energy, because you will be doing what is really important to you and will experience the fulfillment of many accomplishments.

Your Mars will enable you to go after what you want in life, while at the same time appreciating the satisfaction of close personal relationships, and taking other people's well-being into consideration. When you assert yourself, you will be direct and often forceful, but also sensitive to your effect upon others and willing to seriously consider their point

49

of view. You will know that by giving in to others on
minor issues that you will lose little, and that by
compromising occasionally you will develop a mutuality
within your relationships which will enable you to fulfill most of your desires. By being responsive to the
needs of your sexual partner, you will likewise discover that you enhance your own satisfaction as well
as incline your partner to want to please you.

Because your Mars will enable you to assert yourself easily and enjoy the release of physical activity,
you may be inclined to choose an occupation which involves manual labor or which is related to engineering,
mechanics, sports, police work or sales.

JUPITER

*"Man is made by his belief. As he be-
lieves, so he is."*
                    THE BHAGAVAD GITA

*"Nothing is at last sacred but the in-
tegrity of your own mind."*
                    RALPH WALDO EMERSON

*"It is not how much we receive but how
much we can internalize that accounts
for our capacity to grow."*
                    SWAMI RUDRANANDA

*"Our growth doesn't wither other people
around us; it incites others to do the
same."*   ANAIS NIN

*"Man is pushed from below by his drives
but pulled from above by his striving
for meaning."*   VICTOR FRANKL

Negative Expression

If Jupiter is the focal planet of your t-square,
you may be somewhat overconfident and proud, inclined

to overextend and overcommit yourself because you believe so fully in your own capacity to achieve the impossible. Your blind optimism and your happy-go-lucky
attitude may also incline you to exercise poor judgment in matters pertaining to the future. Too often,
you overlook immediate realities and turn your attention to future plans and dreams which you are not
likely to be able to fulfill until you have dealt with
matters at hand. You may even travel incessantly, not
only for enjoyment, but also in order to avoid dealing
with the issues of your daily life.

Physically, your excessive approach to life may
result in weight gain and liver disorders. Psychologically, your lack of moderation leads you to become
carried away with your experiences, activities and relationships. Frequently self-indulgent, lazy and extra-
vagant, you tend to substitute quantity for quality,
taking in more and more pleasurable experiences until
you become congested. Likewise, you expect too much
from other people, demanding that they fulfill your
needs and satisfy your voracious appetites. Although
you are a giver as well as a taker, your giving is
often compulsive, indulgent or patronizing; you boost
your own ego by showering your favors upon people whom
you may regard as inferior or incapable of satisfying
their own needs.

Your focal Jupiter indicates that your restless
search for answers may lead you to become the perpetual student, the searcher who is always looking outside himself, or who doesn't stop his quest long
enough to assimilate what he has learned or to apply
his understanding to his daily life. Or, you may become a know-it-all, possessing the answer to every
question, and philosophically extricating yourself
from every predicament. As a self-proclaimed preacher,
you may dogmatically and self-righteously assert the
truths that you have discovered, but make little attempt to live by your own wisdom.

Positive Expression

Once you have learned to harmoniously express
your Jupiter, your confidence will spring from your

abilities to remain in touch with your own inner teacher or guide, and to apply the insights you gain from your experience and study to every area of your life. You will not allow the heights of understanding which you occasionally reach to inflate your ego, for you will know that these heights remain accessible to all, and you will remain humbly aware of all that you do not yet understand. Able to give from your abundance, you will enrich the lives of others, helping them tap the sources of their own wisdom rather than rely upon you for inspiration and guidance. Although you will adhere to your own truths, you will allow others the freedom to discover and follow their truths, and will respect their insights, whether or not they accord with your own.

Your Jupiter will enable you to function within limits which you, whenever possible, define for yourself, because you will know the inner freedom which results from committing yourself to a purpose in which you fully believe. Yet you will not blindly follow any path which appears in front of you; you will carefully examine each possibility, acting only on those which accord with your own inner voice. You will understand that growth does not necessarily mean endless proliferation, like a cancer which uncontrollably devours all cells within reach; you will know that the quality of your involvement in each experience matters more than a quantity of experiences, and that every "yes" you say to one alternative must also be a "no" to another alternative. You will be a student and a seeker, but rather than live a life of ceaseless wandering, you will allow yourself resting places on your journey - periods of assimilation, moments or months of quiet in which you are free to *find* and to experience the joys of finding.

Your approach to life will be positive and optimistic, not because you are unaware of or insensitive to suffering, but because you have experienced pain in yourself and others, and are aware that even the most difficult circumstances can lead to deeper understanding and constructive action. Your optimism will be grounded, enabling you to reach out to new experiences

without overextending yourself or making empty pro-
mises; you will be aware of your own limitations and
those of others, but will nevertheless maintain your
faith in the future and in human nature. You will
attract wealth - spiritually, emotionally, intellectually and materially, to the extent that you remain
attuned to and give from your own inner wealth.

Professionally, you may gravitate toward occupations related to psychology, law, publishing, education or religion, and may find satisfaction in any
work which enables you to teach, travel, counsel or
operate in a promotional capacity. Whatever you do,
you will want to give generously, protectively and
wisely to others, furthering their development while
at the same time expanding your own capabilities and
insights.

SATURN

*"Where love is lacking, work becomes a
substitute; where work is lacking, love
becomes an opiate."*
        ALICE LYTTENS

*"To love one person I must neglect
another. To follow one path, I must
leave another unexplored."*
        SAM KEEN

*"No work of importance that one's heart
is bent upon with singleminded devotion
will remain unfinished."*
        LAMA GOVINDA

*"Be ye lamps unto yourselves. Be ye a
refuge unto yourselves....Look not for
refuge in anyone besides yourselves."*
        THE UPANISHADS

Negative Expression

If Saturn is the focal planet of your t-square,
you may experience bouts of depression as a result of

your negative attitudes and your harsh demands upon yourself. You may frequently feel overcome with anxiety, worry, loneliness, fear and guilt. Your pessimistic tendencies may incline you to retreat into yourself, exercising a rigid control over your feelings, and to drive yourself to work unceasingly, in the hope of at least experiencing the satisfaction of your accomplishments. But because you are so perfectionistic, you may not be able to fulfill your own expectations. Most likely, a strained relationship with your father has driven you to prove to him that you can be successful, but since you are not content with yourself, even the greatest success brings you little happiness.

Although you are capable of handling even the most difficult of tasks, your desire to gain mastery over your feelings and your external circumstances may incline you to act as ruthlessly with others as you do with yourself - seeking to control them, expressing little sensitivity to their feelings and needs, and denying them satisfaction. As a workaholic, you may restrict the boundaries of your life to the realms of work and material security, denying yourself the rich pleasures of close personal relationships and creative leisure.

You are overly cautious in your relationships, holding yourself apart because you are afraid of intimacy. Although you tend to focus upon few people and to make long-term commitments rather than cultivate a myriad of acquaintances, you prefer security and structure to depth and richness in personal contact. As a result, you are perpetually dissatisfied; you feel deprived and unfulfilled, and turn even more to your work, which cannot fulfill all of your needs. The more restricted you feel, the more melancholy you become, and the more you doubt your capacity to give and receive love, or to experience inner peace.

Your rigid approach to life may even manifest on a physical level, creating back trouble, or problems with the skin, knees, joints or teeth.

Positive Expression

When you have mastered your focal Saturn, you will work diligently and enjoy your accomplishments without being bound by a need to achieve or to prove that you are a success. Attuned to your conscience and aware of your deepest values, you will organize your life around a clearly defined system of priorities; you will make sure that each mountain that you climb is worth climbing and that the process of achieving your professional goals is fulfilling and enriches rather than detracts from the rest of your life.

Likewise, you will experience your self-chosen routines, duties and commitments as liberating as well as stabilizing, because they provide enduring satisfaction and free you to invest your energy in tasks which are important to you. Able to focus singlemindedly upon each of these tasks, you will not allow yourself to be distracted by other alternatives. You will demonstrate patience, concentration and a keen sense of timing as you courageously confront each obstacle, persevering until the work is completed. However, you will refuse to remain enslaved by tasks or structures which are no longer meaningful, and will be able to break away from such external sources of security because you will have built a strong foundation within yourself.

As an autonomous and self-disciplined adult, you will be grounded, practical and realistic, capable of conforming, when necessary, to external circumstances, but without allowing any mountain which you are climbing in the outer world to take precedence over the ascent of your "inner Everest". Your greatest challenge will be of your own development; you will take pride in learning how to cope with anxiety, guilt, loneliness and fear, rather than in suppressing such feelings or allowing them to overpower you. You will discover that by remaining in contact with your feelings, you actually increase your control over your life. Because you will neither deny your own pain nor let it poison you, you will learn from it and become more sensitive to the pain of others.

Your Saturn, at its best, will enable you to cautiously and selectively form close and committed relationships and to work at resolving interpersonal conflicts, knowing that the bonds of your relationships will deepen as each problem is resolved. You will discover that the willingness to share vulnerabilities and weaknesses is more of a strength than the ability to hide them, and you will learn that you can fully touch another person - emotionally, physically, intellectually and spiritually - without losing yourself. Even your relationship with your father will improve, because you will respect his point of view without having to live according to his expectations.

Living now according to your own high but realistic expectations, you will accept your inadequacies and forgive yourself for your mistakes, secure in your awareness that you are a worthy human being and that you are attempting to actively live a full, purposeful, accomplished and well-balanced life.

You will gravitate toward business, government or real estate occupations, or any work which entails responsibility, and in which you can function autonomously, experiencing the satisfaction of successfully confronting daily challenges.

URANUS

"The supreme, the most faultless, largest law of action is to find out the truth of your own highest and inmost existence and live in it and not to follow any external standards."
  MAHATMA GANDHI

"Whoso would be a man must be a nonconformist...Absolve you to yourself, and you shall have the suffrage of the world." *RALPH WALDO EMERSON*

"If a man does not keep pace with his companion, perhaps it is because he

56

hears a different drummer. Let him step
to the music which he hears, however
measured or far away."
            HENRY DAVID THOREAU

"I say unto you: one must still have
chaos within oneself to give birth to
a dancing star."
            FREDERICK NIETZSCHE

"Come to a limit and transcend it; come
to a limit and transcend it. Our only
security is our ability to change."
            JOHN LILLY

Negative Expression

If Uranus is the focal planet of your t-square,
you are attracted to people, activities and circumstances which are unconventional, dramatic and frequently
disruptive. Because you crave excitement, you often
function in an extreme manner, making sudden and sometimes inexplicable changes in your life which throw
you and your relationships out of balance. The frenzied
manner in which you live may even affect your bodily
functioning, resulting in nervous disorders, cramps or
spasms that reflect the instability of your own psyche.

You are motivated by a need to be different from
other people. As a result, you shun normal behaviors
and pursuits and cultivate a lifestyle which many people would regard as bizarre. If red is a popular color
one season, you wear green; if green is popular, you
wear red. You rebel not only because you enjoy rebelling, but also because your contrariness enables you
to shock others and to maintain your belief that because you are so unique, you are somehow better than
anyone else.

You are a person who must live by your own laws,
but because you have spent your life being the opposite
of what other people wanted you to be, you have not
discovered the laws of your own nature. As a result,

you follow your impulses and call that freedom, oppose any rules or restrictions which interfere with your will, and act in an often unpredictable, irresponsible and unreliable manner. But license, which you consider to be freedom, interferes with the freedom of others; your erratic actions upset their equilibrium and disrupt their attempts to maintain stability and self-direction.

Because you oppose restrictions of any kind, you are unable to commit yourself to a person or an activity which you value. You will not tolerate the demands other people make upon your time and energy, and few people will tolerate your idiosyncratic behavior. As a result, you may remain detached in personal relationships, experience many breaks or separations, and/or involve yourself with people who, like you, are determined to remain uncommitted. Frequently, you feel alienated from the people around you.

You claim to be humanitarian, but you neither love yourself nor humanity. Your fanatic nature inclines you to become involved with radical ideas and causes which are not only impractical, but which lead to upheaval and the destruction of established structures, rather than constructive and enduring change.

Positive Expression

When you have learned to express the positive dimension of your focal Uranus, you will be an individualist, capable of following your own unique path while at the same time respecting the needs of others and forming enduring relationships. Interdependent as well as independent, you will be aware of how other people can contribute to your welfare, and will likewise be inclined to aid them in their own self-actualization. In touch with the bonds that link you to others, you will be a friend to humanity, not only espousing the rights of the poor or downtrodden, but also exhibiting kindness, tolerance and warmth in your personal relationships.

You will enjoy being different from the people around you, but will know that having to be different is as limiting as having to conform. By remaining in touch with the laws of your inner being, you will be free either to adapt to your environment or to strike out on your own, as each situation requires. If you must rebel, then you will rebel against the injustice of society by showing what an aware, evolved, sensitive and capable human being you can become, despite all the obstacles on your self-chosen path.

Your Uranus will incline you to be an original and experimental thinker, courageously opening yourself to new ideas while at the same time valuing the usefulness of old ideas and established structures. Humanitarian by nature, you will be an advocate of psychological and social reform. You will promote change, committing yourself to that cause or movement which is the most constructive and practical, but will not seek to tear down the old without being able and willing to replace it with something more viable. Whether as a psychologist, astrologer, inventor, scientist or technician, your primary task will be that of an awakener; you will disrupt patterns of thought and behavior that operate around you, but only when you are able to awaken human consciousness to new patterns which are infinitely more liberating.

As an agent of change, you will also instigate changes in your own life, but only after you have made sure that the old patterns must be destroyed or reawakened if you are to continue furthering your own development. Your prime target of change will be your inner self, for you will be fully aware that the only truly successful revolution is an internal revolution. You will be able to meet head-on the forces which obstruct you, and to expand your consciousness wide enough to allow new possibilities of understanding and action to unfold.

Continually stimulated by your own psyche and your environment, you will be open to flashes of intuition and insight which will enable you to transcend the polarities and paradoxes of your existence, and to experience and remain in touch with universal laws. Careful not to confuse your own small will with the universal will, you will allow your intuition to pass the test of reality and the test of time. The laws that you live by will expand your sense of inner freedom; likewise, you will understand that structures, limits and commitments that are self-chosen, in which your path is aligned with the greater path set out for you, are also liberating. Because you will experience spiritual and psychological freedom, you will not always be asserting a need for freedom which sets your will against the wills of others. Because your will includes an awareness of other people's will, you will direct yourself toward their fulfillment as well as your own.

Uranus, as the planet of change, will teach you to cope with the unexpected circumstances in your life, and to trust that the new developments that disrupt your previous lifestyle will in time reveal their purpose and source of gain. Because you will hold onto your own inner foundations rather than any external security, you will not lose yourself when you leave behind relationships, jobs or possessions which once were important to you. You will know that your security is your complete acceptance of your ultimate insecurity, and will be prepared to cope with changes in your personal life that may shake your foundations temporarily, but will also open your awareness to new insights and new paths of action.

NEPTUNE

"Not till we are lost...do we begin to find ourselves." HENRY DAVID THOREAU

"Never retain in the world of imagination (the ideal that) can be brought into reality." SWAMI RUDRANANDA

"Any time you think you need healing, heal someone else....Whenever you are confused and troubled, stop to think: "Where have I failed to give?" MICHIO KUSHI

*"Within man is the soul of the whole;
the wise silence; the universal beauty,
to which every part and particle is
equally related; the eternal One...Only
by the vision of that Wisdom can the
horoscope of the ages be read...can we
know what it saith."*
                    RALPH WALDO EMERSON

Negative Expression

If Neptune is the focal planet of your t-square,
you are frequently lost in a dream world of your own
creation. Carried away with illusions and unrealistic
expectations, you escape from realities which require
an investment of energy and seek contentment fantasi-
zing about the ideal rather than attempting to actualize it.

Passively, you drift through life, absorbing the
thoughts and feelings of other people without filtering them through your own psyche. Oversensitive because you take in more impressions than you can assimilate, you exist in a perpetual fog, unable to think
clearly - to sort out reality and fantasy or to separate your thoughts and feelings from the thoughts and
feelings of others. As a result, you often feel paralyzed, incapable of acting decisively. Your lack of
clarity about yourself leads you to deceive yourself
and others, expressing yourself indirectly and sometimes deviously, because you do not know your own mind
and heart.

This passivity which you so often experience may
lead you to become overly dependent upon drugs or alcohol, or to blindly become a follower in a movement
which appeals to your emotions. It may incline you to
form parasitical relationships in which you are overly
acquiescent and allow yourself to be exploited, all
the while deluding yourself that you are merging with
the other. You may place yourself in a sacrificial
role, giving yourself too freely to a job, cause or
person in order to demonstrate your selflessness. In a

close relationship, you may fall in love with what you regard to be the potential of your weak or suffering loved one, and then become disillusioned and bitter when your help is not appreciated, or when the other person does not turn out to be as ideal as you had envisioned.

Your afflicted Neptune may also influence your health, resulting in an oversensitivity to foods and medicines, as well as psychosomatic illnesses which can neither be diagnosed nor healed by conventional means. You may also be susceptible to hepatitis or paralysis.

Positive Expression

When you have learned to express the highest dimensions of your focal Neptune, you will know how to dispel the fog which so often envelops you by centering yourself and contacting your source of inner light. A natural mystic, you will meditate frequently, experiencing moments of oneness and harmony with the universe, illuminating moments which will deepen your faith and enable you to be an inspirational and healing influence upon others. You will be able to find inspiration in the most mundane details of your life, because you will cultivate a spirituality which infiltrates your daily life rather than exists apart from it. If the spiritual is not your path, then you will discover your purpose in social service or in the creative arts. Through helping the poor, the troubled or the ill, you may satisfy your call to serve humanity. Through music, literature, film or photography, you may channel your creative energies into finished works of art, rather than allow those energies to remain unexpressed and to wreak havoc upon your psyche.

Your visionary abilities will enable you to use the powers of your imagination for the benefit of yourself and others, creating vivid and positive thought forms which can constructively influence events in the external world. Rather than be victim of the undisciplined flights of your imagination, you will examine each vision or direction you conceive of in the light of reality, carefully considering its importance to you, the sacrifice it entails, and the relationship between its means and its ends. You will carefully assess each tide before you surrender to it, examining each relationship before you invest yourself emotionally and each activity or cause before you make a commitment. Devoting yourself only to those paths which accord with your own inner vision and which have practical application, you will translate into reality those ideals which will emotionally, physically, intellectually and spiritually enrich you and other people. Your life will be infused with meaning because you will be actualizing a purpose which transcends yourself.

In your personal and work relationships, you will be accepting, receptive and compassionate without cultivating dependency; you will, when necessary, refuse to fulfill desires of others which are detrimental to your welfare and theirs. In love, you will be careful not to delude yourself that each attachment you form is a soul-mate connection and each person your perfect mate. Because you will be able to love from the highest dimensions of yourself, you will form bonds which are deep, firm, uplifting and mutually strengthening.

Aware of your oversensitive and psychic nature and the ease with which you absorb the feelings of others, you will learn to protect yourself from negative energy by avoiding contact with people who drain or poison you psychologically. You will allow yourself periods of quiet and meditation in which you regain contact with your feelings and experience the clarity and illumination that results from flowing with the highest energies of the universe.

PLUTO

"In the empty spaces - lacunae, vacuums, pauses, voids, black holes...new things begin.... (We are born anew) from the unexplored spaces, the badlands, the outlaw territory."   SAM KEEN

"To arrive where you are, to get from where you are not,/You must go by a way wherein there is no ecstacy.../In order to possess what you do not possess/You must go by the way of dispossession./In order to arrive at what you are not/You must go through the way in which you are not."   T.S. ELIOT

"So the darkness shall be the light, and the stillness the dancing."
          T.S. ELIOT

"All the gods and demons, the forces of light and darkness are within us....Those who want to conquer the Lord of Death will have to meet him and to recognize him in the midst of life."
          LAMA GOVINDA

"We cannot avoid using power....So let us...love powerfully."   MARTIN BUBER

Negative Expression

Your t-square to Pluto indicates that you are a remote and private person who refuses to allow other people access to the turbulent underworld of your psyche. The battles occurring within you are so intense that you either deny your desires and passions and function on minimal energy, or you erupt like a volcano, exploding into often cruel and destructive behaviors.

Once you release the turmoil within you, you are often ruthless in satisfying your desires. You may become enslaved by sexual or material obsessions, seeking revenge against those people you feel have harmed you, dominating and exploiting those who cannot stand up to your power, or using your keen perceptiveness of others to manipulate them into satisfying your needs.

Too easily, you allow the dark forces within to overcome you. Unable or unwilling to find constructive outlets for your pent-up energy, you allow it to drive you to extremes. Every experience must be intense and transforming, every action motivated by your all-or-nothing approach to life. Because you view the world through black and white lenses, you can neither accept other people nor yourself. Your judgment is harsh. All that does not conform to your wishes or your perceptions of reality must be pushed, forced or compelled to undergo drastic changes.

Because you feel powerless in controlling the demons that rage within you, you attempt to wield power over other people. But your power is ineffectual, because no matter how successfully you dominate others, you are still at the mercy of your own psyche.

Positive Expression

When you have learned to harness and channel your Plutonian energies, you will be able to experience the darkness at your core without allowing it to overcome or deform you. You will discover that contacting and accepting those primal forces enables you to draw from an illimitable supply of energy and personal power, to cope with major crises, to regenerate yourself when drained or discouraged, and to involve yourself with total commitment in an activity, cause or relationship which deserves your investment of energy.

When you discharge the energy at the nucleus of your being, you will not explode destructively; you will be able to contain that energy, and to transmute it into constructive activity. Aware of its potency, you will find adequate releases for it in your daily life - connecting emotionally with other people, experiencing sexual heights which are mutually fulfilling, and confronting challenges in your personal life and in your work.

Your ability to venture into the underworld of your psyche will enable you to help others handle their emotional conflicts. Because you will be able to absorb

your own shadow, you will not fear theirs; your acceptance of their dark side will help them to accept themselves, and to likewise contact their own vast resources and transform their darkness into light. In
touch with your inner power, you will not need to
wield power in your relationships; you will be aware
of your effect upon other people and will not allow
yourself to manipulate them for your own benefit. Your
influence will be healing and penetrating. Because you
will journey far into your own depths, you will perceive the depths in others; as a born investigator,
you will also be able to penetrate the mysteries of
the world around you.

Your desire to venture beneath the surface of
inner or outer reality may lead you to become a detective, archaeologist, physicist or occultist. Adept at
working with other people's material resources, you
may find your calling as a banker, fund-raiser, insurance agent or grant administrator; adept at working
with their emotional, physical or intellectual resources, you may become a psychologist, doctor, researcher or editor. Because of your courage in facing
death or illness, you may be one of the hardy few willing to work with the dead or dying.

You will live deeply and intensely, but will also
be able to relax and enjoy quiet pleasures because you
will have discovered effective outlets for your vast
energy and will not be at the mercy of its insistent
need to be released. However, you will also experience
periods of transformation during which you feel as if
you have died and been reborn; these experiences will
tear you apart but also strengthen you, fusing you into a new whole and enabling you again and again to be
revitalized by the healing energies within you.

FOCAL PLANET POSITIONS

When birth time is known, the house placement is indicated. If the focal planet is between signs or houses, both signs or houses are specified. A listing of two planets indicates a focal planet conjunction.

T-SQUARE TO THE SUN

Richard Alpert-☉/♅ ♈ **1**
Lucille Ball-♌
Harry Belafonte-☉/♃ ♓
Jack Benny-♒ **2**
Marlon Brando-☉/☽ ♈ **4/5**
Bette Davis-♈ **3**
Galileo-♓
Liberace-☉/♂ ♉ **4**
Ronald Reagan-♒
Vanessa Redgrave-♒
Dylan Thomas-♏
Yogananda-♑

T-SQUARE TO THE MOON

Richard Alpert-♐**6**
Ray Bradbury-♐
Marlon Brando-☉/☽ ♈ **4/5**
Walt Disney-♎**1**
Bobby Fischer-♉ **10**
Mahatma Gandhi-♌ **10**
Hermann Hesse-☽/♄ ♓ **3**
Martin Luther King-♓
Edna St. V. Millay-♐**7**
Liza Minelli-☽/♂/♄ ♋ **3/4**
Paul Simon-♋ **12**
Oscar Wilde-♌ **12**

T-SQUARE TO MERCURY

Spiro Agnew-♐
W.H. Auden-☿/♄ ♓
A.C. Doyle-☿/♇ ♉
Patty Hearst-☿/♀ ♓ **7**
Aldous Huxley-♋
Herman Melville-♍
Henry Moore-♍
Fritz Perls-♌ **1**
Wilhelm Reich-♓ **1**
Richard Wagner-♉

T-SQUARE TO VENUS

Woody Allen-♎
Albert Camus-♎ **1/2**
Betty Friedan-♈**3**
John Glenn-♊**7**
Patty Hearst-☿/♀ ♓ **7**
Willie Mays-♀/♅ ♈
Claude Monet-♀/♄ ♐
Mary Tyler Moore-♐**9**
Anais Nin-♓ **6**
George Sand-♌ **6**

T-SQUARE TO MARS

Muhammed Ali-♉ **9**
Johnny Carson-♎ **12**
Colette-♏**1**
Adelle Davis-♂/♃ ♓ **3**
Erich Fromm-♓
Indira Gandhi-♍**1**
Helen Hayes-♌ **1**
Ernest Hemingway-♍ **1**
Liberace-☉/♂ ♉
Henry Mancini-♑ **1**
Thomas Jefferson-♌
Liza Minelli-♂/♄/☽ ♋ **3/4**
Aristotle Onassis-♍**10**
Dr. Seuss-♂/♃ ♈

T-SQUARE TO JUPITER

Harry Belafonte-☉/♃♓
Annie Besant-☽/♃♋
Glen Campbell-♐**2**
Julius Caesar-♓
Adelle Davis-♂/♃♓**3**
Betty Ford-♊**9**
Judy Garland-♃/♄♎**4**
George Gershwin-♍
Immanuel Kant-♒
Grace Metalious-♐**2**
Norman Mailer-♏
Guru Maharaji-♃/♆♏**1**
Eleanor Roosevelt-♌**9**
Dr. Seuss-♂/♃♈
Barbra Streisand-♊**3**
William Wordsworth-♐

T-SQUARE TO SATURN

W.H. Auden-☿/♄♓
Fidel Castro-♐
Charles deGaulle-♍
Judy Garland-♃/♄♎**4**
Allen Ginsberg-♏
Hugh Hefner-♏
Hermann Hesse-☽/♄♓
Lyndon Johnson-♈**4**
Christine Jorgenssen-♏**2/3**
James Joyce-♉**5**
Karl Marx-♄/♇♓
Liza Minelli-♂/♄/☽♋**3/4**
Claude Monet-♀/♄♐
Marilyn Monroe-♏**4**
Nelson Rockefeller-♈**6**
Theodore Roosevelt-♌

T-SQUARE TO URANUS

Richard Alpert-☉/♅♈**11**
Neil Armstrong-♈**11/12**
Isaac Asimov-♒
Thomas Becket-♌
Emily Bronte-♐
Winston Churchill-♌**11**
Kahlil Gibran-♍**1**
Gurdjieff-♌**10/11**
Willie Mays-♀/♅♈
Sylvia Plath-♈**1**
Rudolph Steiner-♊
Thomas Wolfe-♈

T-SQUARE TO NEPTUNE

Ludwig Beethoven-♍
Lord Byron-♎
Walter Cronkite-♄/♆♌
Art Garfunkel-♍**2**
Henry Kissinger-♌**3**
Guru Maharaji-♃/♆♏**1**
Henry Matisse-♈
Artur Rimbaud-♓**5**
Helena Rubinstein-♈**3**
Tchaikovsky-♒
Voltaire-♓

T-SQUARE TO PLUTO

Brigitte Bardot-♋**8**
Anita Bryant-♌**12**
Evangeline Adams-♉**2**
A.C. Doyle-☿/♇♉
Katherine Hepburn-♊
John Lennon-♌**10**
Shirley MacLaine-♋**10**
Karl Marx-♄/♇♓
Ralph Nader-♋**7**
Florence Nightingale-♓**7**
Gloria Steinem-♋**9**
Henry Thoreau-♓

FOCAL SIGNS

In order to utilize the energy of your t-square beneficially, you must first be aware of the constructive expression of its planets, signs and houses. This chapter contains tables which indicate the positive and negative manifestations of signs. Because the sign of your focal planet is so highly energized, it may express itself more powerfully in your life than any other sign in your chart. Therefore, it is particularly important that you familiarize yourself with both its favorable and unfavorable characteristics.

These tables can be applied not only to the focal sign of your t-square, but also to the other signs in your chart, whether they contain planets or merely occupy a house. If you want to begin to develop the positive qualities of the empty space of your t-square, you must first understand the possible manifestations of the empty sign.

A sign, like a planet, may function negatively if you allow it to operate: a) unconsciously, without cultivating its positive expression, b) in an extreme manner, c) inappropriately, and d) without the awareness and integration of other parts of yourself, particularly the parts indicated by the opposite sign of the zodiac ' A vice is often the *exaggeration, misapplication* or *compulsive operation* of a virtue. The signs in your chart can indicate your virtues if you consciously attempt to express their positive qualities in moderation and in the appropriate circumstances, integrating their expression with the constructive expression of their opposite signs.

Because the focal sign of your t-square is over-emphasized, the body parts or functions related to that sign (as well as to the focal planet) may be overactive and experience considerable tension, leading to illness. The body parts or functions related to the sign of the empty space, which may be under-developed or weak, will be affected by such malfunctioning. The following chart indicates the physiological correspondences of each sign of the zodiac:

ARIES - *head, brain, upper jaw, blood, muscles, pituitary gland (also adrenal glands?)*
TAURUS - *neck, throat, lower jaw, upper esophagus, thyroid gland, metabolic system*
GEMINI - *arms, hands, shoulders, lungs, upper ribs, nerves, thymus gland, respiratory system*
CANCER - *stomach, upper alimentary canal, salivary glands, breasts, uterus, menstruation*
LEO - *heart, spinal cord, upper back, spleen*
VIRGO - *small intestine, abdomen, gall bladder, pancreas, lower alimentary canal*
LIBRA - *kidneys, adrenal glands, endocrine glands, ovaries, appendix*
SCORPIO - *colon, bladder, eliminative system, male reproductive system*
SAGITTARIUS - *hips, thighs, buttocks, liver, lower spine, autonomic nervous system*
CAPRICORN - *bones, teeth, knees, joints, skin, hair, skeletal system, sebaceous glands*
AQUARIUS - *ankles, calves, nerves, parathyroid glands, circulatory system*
PISCES - *feet, body fluids, lymphatic system, lachrymal glands*

ARIES

Positive Expression	*Negative Expression*
initiating, pioneering, capable of new beginnings enterprising	impulsive, hasty, impatient, seeks immediate satisfaction, lacks foresight and follow-through
direct, straightforward, spontaneous, honest, open	tactless, uncontrolled, unaware, unreceptive
self-directed, self-motivated, self-reliant, independent, individualistic, confident, born leader	headstrong, me-first attitude, uncooperative
risk-taking, courageous	rash, reckless, careless foolhardy
energetic, dynamic, outgoing	competitive, dominating, domineering
active, accomplishing	restless, hyperactive, directionless
assertive, confrontative	aggressive, argumentative, combative, contentious, pushy, quick-tempered
enthusiastic, optimistic, exuberant, eager, idealistic	overly excitable, immoderate, impractical
stimulating, exciting, energizing, passionate	agitating, overly intense, high-powered, exhausting
creative, inspiring	simplistic, black and white
personal, personally involved, self-expressive	self-absorbed, egotistical, narcissistic

71

TAURUS

Positive Expression	*Negative Expression*
loyal, devoted, warm, affectionate, faithful, trustworthy	possessive, jealous, overly attached
practical, respectful of tradition, conserving	ultraconservative, conformist, craves security
self-sufficient, concerned with earning capacity	materialistic, stingy, money-grubbing, unspiritual
productive, resourceful, managerial	overly concerned with the material or tangible
patient, persistent, thorough, resolute, strong-willed, determined, concentrated energy, fixed purpose	slow, plodding, stubborn, bullheaded, obstinate, won't ever give up
stable, steady, solid, reliable, constant firm, enduring	immovable, unchanging, dull, boring
artistic	unoriginal, conventional
easygoing, "down home" temperament	lazy, inert
earthy, sensual, pleasure-loving	self-indulgent, greedy, acquisitive, carnal, gluttonous, lascivious, dissolute
concerned with values, worth, quality	values only physical and material satisfactions
values self, has self esteem	overemphasizes own worth or lack of worth

GEMINI

Positive Expression	Negative Expression
versatile, diverse, multifaceted, varied, possessing many skills	scattered, dabbling, superficial, ambivalent, inconsistent, double-dealing, two-faced
mobile, lively	changeable, mercurial, inconstant, unreliable, unsteady
agile, quick, alert, dexterous, facile	nervous, restless, speedy, highstrung, fidgety, lacking concentration
sociable, interactive, congenial, adaptable	uncommitted, fickle, flighty, capricious
inquisitive, curious	concerned with trivia, imitative
logical, rational, scientific, synthesizing	overly logical, rationalizing, unfeeling, detached
knowledgeable, informative, mentally stimulating	shallow, unphilosophical, lacking purpose or depth of understanding, amoral
verbal, literary, skilled with words, articulate, eloquent	verbose, loquacious, chattering, gossipy, glib
clever, witty, amusing	tricky, sly, manipulative, cunning, scheming, dishonest
living in the present	mired in immediate realities, loss of perspective

CANCER

Positive Expression	Negative Expression
maternal, nurturing, protective, nourishing	smothering, suffocating, possessive, indulgent, pampering
sensitive, soft-hearted, deeply feeling	hypersensitive, touchy, easily hurt, thin-skinned, crybaby, maudlin, delicate, overly impressionable
psychic, intuitive, attuned to the unconscious	overly emotional, moody, emotionally insecure, hysterical, brooding
sympathetic, empathetic, receptive, responsive, comforting, supportive, consoling	overly responsive, craves being needed, loses self in others, symbiotic
loyal, devoted, tenacious	clinging, parasitic, dependent, timid, passive
childlike, innocent	childish, needy, helpless
rooted, domestic, family-oriented, appreciative of the past	clannish, reclusive, stay-at-home, provincial, clings to the past
self-protective, cautious	secretive, withheld, withdrawn, self-absorbed
self-effacing	martyr-like, self-pitying, pathetic
shrewd, thrifty	selfish

LEO

Positive Expression	*Negative Expression*
confident, self-assured, self-possessed, self-aware, self-respecting	self-worshiping, ego-centric, self-important, cocksure, inflated, conceited, boastful
dignified, influential prestigious, capable of managing or leading	arrogant, haughty, pompous, snobbish, status-conscious
commanding, powerful, determined, strong-willed	overpowering, dominating, power-mad, autocratic, overbearing, dictatorial
generous, benevolent, magnanimous	patronizing, conde-scending, extravagant, indulgent, pampering
affectionate, warm, loyal, faithful, romantic	"Don Juan," swayed by flattery, flirtatious, needs excessive love, demands admiration and appreciation
playful, spontaneous, genuine, fun-loving, optimistic, buoyant, high-spirited	childish, self-indulgent, always playing, incapable of being serious
creative, self-expressive, entertaining, dramatic	melodramatic, show-off, ostentatious, must be center stage, always role-playing

VIRGO

Positive Expression	*Negative Expression*
exacting, methodical, detailed	narrow, picky, petty, trivial
orderly, organized, meticulous, systematic	overly organized, overly fastidious, highly structured
diligent, industrious, efficient, thorough, conscientious, studious	perfectionistic, always busy, workaholic, drudging, self-exploiting, incapable of relaxing
constructively critical	hypercritical, self-critical, carping, unaccepting
discriminating, selective	overly particular, fussy, finicky, perpetually dissatisfied, prudish
analytical, mentally sharp, mentally processing	overly analytical, overly skeptical, always dis-secting, separative
concerned	worrying, focusing upon the negative, anxious
modest, unassuming	timid, self-deprecating
helpful, useful, obliging, responsible, dependable, assisting	servile, self-prostitu-ting, menial, subservient, slavishly submissive, ingratiating
health-conscious	hypochondriacal, complain-ing, fanatical about diet

LIBRA

Positive Expression	*Negative Expression*
relationship-oriented, sociable	other-centered, dependent, flirtatious
sharing, cooperating, mediating	overly compromising
pleasing, agreeable, likeable, charming, hospitable	overly accommodating, placifying, compliant, acquiescent, docile
diplomatic, tactful	phony, dishonest, unreal, flattering, pretending
peace-loving, harmonious	avoiding conflict, seeks peace at any price
suave, poised, elegant, refined	overemphasizing appearances, vain, pseudo-sophisticated
artistic, good taste, cultured, aesthetic, beauty-conscious	superficial values, frivolous, aesthetic snobbery, overemphasizing form
evaluating, weighing, seeking perspective, objective, aware of all points of view	vacillating, indecisive, wishy-washy, fence-sitting, contradictory
striving for balance	oscillating, fluctuating, up and down, extremist
fair, just, striving for equality	defines "fairness" for own benefit, unable to accept reality

SCORPIO

Positive Expression	*Negative Expression*
intense, passionate	overly intense, lustful, violent
loyal, deeply feeling, steadfast in adversity	possessive, jealous, unforgiving, resentful, revengeful, vindictive
strong, courageous, capable of confronting and channelling powerful emotions	demonic, morbid, brooding, wallowing, thrives on suffering
determined, strong-willed, staying power, enduring	willful, unyielding, obsessive, ruthless
self-disciplined, controlled	repressed, controlling
thorough, responsible	all-or-nothing, extremist
penetrating, probing, investigating, shrewd, resourceful, profound, insightful	prying, scheming, exploitative, using insights gained for selfish purposes
magnetic, enigmatic, mysterious, self-protective	hidden, secretive, closed
truthful	sharp, cruel, sarcastic
regenerating, healing	destructive, subversive, injurious
stoical, able to eliminate inessentials	self-denying, judgmental

SAGITTARIUS

Positive Expression	*Negative Expression*
purposeful, singleminded, goal-directed, aspiring	impractical, unrealistic, impatient, "head in the clouds"
prophetic, farsighted, future-oriented, planning	blind to immediate realities
searching, truth-seeking, philosophical, idealistic, openminded, self-improving	ceaselessly speculating, overly abstract, abstruse, self-deluding
wise, profound, discerning, enlightened, well-read, inspired	opinionated, bookish, obscure, pretentious
inspirational, guiding, teaching	didactic, long-winded, imposing one's truth upon others
ethical, principled	moralistic, dogmatic, preachy, intolerant, hypocritical
direct, frank, truthful	blunt, tactless, outspoken
generous, altruistic, amiable, openhearted	wasteful, extravagant, superficially friendly
jovial, buoyant, high-spirited, optimistic, enthusiastic, happy-go-lucky, carefree	blindly optimistic, exaggerating, boisterous, careless, sloppy, irresponsible, unreliable, procrastinating, overextended
exploring, outreaching, freedom-loving, outdoors-oriented	restless, full of wanderlust, can't tolerate restrictions

CAPRICORN

Positive Expression	Negative Expression
serious, earnest, reserved	melancholy, negative, despondent, gloomy, brooding
realistic, practical, economical, thrifty	pessimistic, fatalistic, cynical, materialistic, stingy, miserly
cautious, prudent, keen sense of timing	fearful, distrustful, overly cautious
controlled, self-disciplined, self-contained, self-sufficient, self-reliant, stoical	closed, repressed, inhibited, rigid, misanthropic, insensitive, cruel, severe
loyal, committed, steadfast	resigned, cool, cold, remote, inaccessible
responsible, reliable, scrupulous, fatherly, law-abiding	conservative, ultra-conventional, obsessed with rules/formalities
persistent, persevering, concentrating, patient	slow, tedious
diligent, hard-working, driving, achieving	perfectionistic, driven, narrow, unable to relax
high-reaching, ambitious, enterprising	status-seeking, power-hungry, manipulative, calculating, mercenary
successful, powerful, managerial, executive capability	authoritarian, domineering, exploitative, patronizing

AQUARIUS

Positive Expression	*Negative Expression*
truth-seeking, intellectual, scientific	abstract, coolly logical
friendly, brotherly, humane, kind, people-oriented	impersonal, detached, aloof, distant, remote, uninvolved
tolerant, openminded, unprejudiced	intolerant of intolerance
humanitarian, progressive, reformist, idealistic, concerned, politically active, cause-oriented	radical, revolutionary, utopian, impractical, pseudo-liberal
individualistic, unconventional	rebellious, contrary, unpredictable, erratic
innovative, inventive, original, unique, unusual	eccentric, bizarre, shocking
intuitive, attuned to the universal Will	self-willed, confuses own will with greater Will
determined, resolute	stubborn, inflexible, fixed
independent, freedom-loving	intolerant of restraint, lawless, uncommitted

PISCES

Positive Expression	*Negative Expression*
adaptable, flexible, flowing, surrendering, agreeable, easy to please, mellow	drifting, directionless, lost, easily influenced, acquiescent, compliant, submissive
accepting, tolerant, forgiving, trusting	undiscriminating, uncritical, lenient, imprudent
tender, gentle, kind, sensitive	soft, weak, timid, easily hurt, oversensitive
psychic, intuitive	overly impressionable, unprotected, absorbent
sympathetic, soothing, compassionate, unselfish, giving, sacrificing, devoted	overly responsive, martyr-like, overly sacrificing, dependent, parasitic
humble, unassuming, modest, unpretentious	meek, cowardly, spineless, weak-willed, self-deprecating, self-pitying, easily victimized
introspective, reflective, subtle, elusive	retreating, evasive, indirect, devious, deceptive
synthesizing, wholistic, perceiving the unity or essence	illogical, unanalytical
imaginative, creative, inspired, musical, poetic	daydreaming, impractical, unrealistic, deluded
spiritual, transcendent, inspirational, serene, idealistic, visionary	escapist, "spacy", vague, confused, nebulous, drug or alcohol-addicted, disillusioned, bitter, cynical

OPPOSING SIGNS

One way of easing the conflict you experience as a result of your t-square and gaining control over its expression is to learn to synthesize the opposing planets, signs and houses that occur in your t-square opposition. This chapter is concerned not only with the negative manifestations of opposing signs, but also with their positive manifestations or synthesis. The next chapter discusses the polarities and synthesis of opposing houses. The interpretations provided in these chapters can be applied to the opposition in a t-square, and to any other opposition in a natal chart, particularly if it is angular, close in orb, involving three or more planets, or involving planets in their own signs and houses. Such oppositions include not only oppositions between planets, but also oppositions indicated by the signs of the ascendant/descendant axis, the midheaven/nadir axis and the lunar nodal axis.

If you have a t-square in your chart, the material included here on synthesis can also help you to understand and develop the sign of your empty space and to integrate it with the sign of your focal planet. Such integration cannot occur until you have first encountered and invited into your life the energies of the empty sign, and until have begun to outwardly express these energies.

Because there are forty-one possible combinations of planets which could occur in opposition in charts of people born in the twentieth century, a thorough study of each of these oppositions and their resulting synthesis would require a book in itself. Therefore, specific interpretations of planets in opposition are not covered here. You may want to consult a text such as Frances Sakoian's *Astrologer's Handbook* or Robert Pelletier's *Planets in Aspect* if you are unable to interpret planetary oppositions. Thinking in terms of your opposing planets existing in conjunction, sextile or trine can help you understand how these planetary energies might be synthesized.

Because the polarities described here are concerned with the signs apart from the planets and houses involved in an opposition, you will have to modify each interpretation as you read it, relating it to the specific planets and houses involved in the opposition which you are interpreting. An opposition between Pluto in Leo in the fifth house and Mars in Aquarius in the eleventh house will, for example, function much differently than an opposition between Neptune in Leo in the twelfth house and Moon in Aquarius in the sixth house. All factors involved in an opposition must be understood and interrelated before they can be synthesized and expressed in a unified and constructive manner.

One side of your opposition may be stronger than the other side if its planet is closer to an angle than the opposing planet, in its own sign or house, or in conjunction. In any of the above circumstances, the influence of the stronger sign prevails over the weaker sign, attempting to dominate it or preventing it from functioning positively. Although the stronger side of your opposition will demand to be expressed, both sides must be expressed and integrated if you are to rise above the pull of conflicting tensions.

If one of your opposing planets is 29 degrees of a sign, the next sign in the zodiac will influence it, and must also be synthesized. If your opposition occurs between planets which are five rather than six signs apart (e.g., Jupiter at 27 Gemini and Moon at 1 1 Capricorn), you will have to apply your own intuition when interpreting the struggle between the two planets and understanding how their signs might be synthesized. Read the sections in chapter three pertaining to the signs in question. Consider how each sign might influence the other. Study material written on inconjuncts (also called quincunxes) by sign, such as is included in chapter five of *Astrology, The Divine Science** by Mark Douglas and Marcia Moore. Determine how the planetary ruler of one sign might function in the sign of the other (e.g., in the previous example, Mercury in Capricorn or Saturn in Gemini), or how the rulers of each sign would manifest in opposition or become integrated in conjunction, sextile or trine (e.g., in the above example, Saturn opposition Mercury, or Saturn conjunct, sextile or trine Mercury).

An opposition between planets six signs apart involves signs of the same quality or mode (cardinal, fixed, or mutable) and tends to exaggerate that quality as well as the similar characteristics of the opposing signs. It also leads the divergent characteristics of each sign to interfere with each other's attempts at expression. For example, an opposition between Taurus and Scorpio indicates powerful will and determination, but the inertia of Taurus interferes with the release or sublimation of energy in Scorpio and the intensity and turmoil of Scorpio upsets the stability and productivity of Taurus.

The section in chapter one on oppositions describes several of the manifestations of oppositions, such as a state of paralysis, fluctuations from one part of oneself to another, denial of one part leading it to operate unconsciously, or the projection of that characteristic onto another person and the waging of one's internal battles externally.

An opposition is also problematic when:

a) the negative characteristics of each polarity are allowed to predominate, and the positive characteristics are not cultivated. (See chapter three, on the positive and negative expressions of signs.)
b) one side is expressed without an awareness of the needs of the other side, or the characteristics of

---

* *a highly recommended text.*

one planet and sign are excessively developed while
the characteristics of the other remain deficient.
c) both sides of the opposition are overly developed
and operate in an extreme manner.
d) each side is expressed inappropriately.
e) one side upsets or interferes with the functioning
of the other.
f) one side manifests in a distorted manner, and is
used to fulfill the questionable purposes of the
other side.

If you have a Taurus/Scorpio opposition, the five
above-mentioned possibilities might operate as follows:

a) You become dominated by your material and sensual
appetites.
b) You vegetate, eating yourself into a stupor or sitting passively in front of the television set, refusing to experience or channel your Scorpionic energies productively.
c) You work two jobs during the week in order to buy a
jaguar, an expensive wardrobe and a yacht, and
spend a passionate weekend in bed with your current
lover.
d) You are lazy at work and accomplish little, but
devour three detective novels every night.
e) Your Taurean materialism keeps you working full-
time as a manager, when you'd have to cut down to
part-time or make substantial material sacrifices
if you were to pursue your desire to become a psychologist.
f) You use your Scorpionic perceptiveness to ferret out
the vulnerabilities of other people, and to manipulate them into buying the low quality products which
you sell on the job.

These are all negative manifestations of an opposition. But an opposition also has a high potential
for awareness, enlightened action and fulfilling relationships. When its two polarities are integrated, you
are able to expand your consciousness, and to perceive
and follow a wide array of alternatives and pathways.
You are able to draw upon energy which was previously
dead-locked by internal battles, and to become more

creative and self-directed in action. When you express both sides of yourself rather than project one part onto others and accuse them of behaviors which you can't bear to see in yourself, you become more objective, more tolerant and more willing to cooperate.

But is a synthesis of opposing planets, signs and houses the answer to transcending the conflicts of your opposition? Perhaps. A fluctuation between the two sides of your nature may be viable for you, if neither side is destructive. A compromise between the two may also be acceptable, although neither side of yourself will be fully satisfied.

In his inspirational book, *Esoteric Astrology*, Dr. Douglas Baker describes the lessons of Libra, a sign similar in meaning to the opposition aspect because it opposes the first sign of the zodiac, Aries. Drawing from the works of Alice Bailey and Robert Assagioli, Baker explains the difference between compromise and synthesis, between:

> *"two kinds of equilibrium: one lower and static; another...high and dynamic....The lower equilibrium can be characterized by the word compromise. This often is a relatively better position and attitude than that of extremes, or than a condition of constant oscillation. But it is apt to induce a state of negativity, of inertia, and in any case it gives no incentive to progress."**

Baker uses the analogy of a point in the middle of a line to describe the state of compromise. The higher equilibrium, however,

> *"brings about a living, dynamic synthesis... The higher equilibrium consists in the <u>control</u> (not suppression, nor neutralization)*

---

* *Baker, Dr. Douglas, ESOTERIC ASTROLOGY, published by Dr. Baker, Herts, England.*

*of the opposing forces, in their <u>wise regulation and use</u> for constructive purposes.
In this case the controlling and regulating
principle dwells on, and operates from a
higher level than that on which the two
opposites are found....The higher equilibrium...corresponds to a triangular relationship."* *

In one of these examples of this triangular relationship, Dr. Baker suggests that the compromise between
excitement and depression is apathy and that the synthesis is serenity.

On a practical level, this triangular relationship can be related directly to oppositions in the
chart and to the t-square configuration as a whole.
Consider the dissatisfaction of a woman with a Taurus/
Scorpio opposition who is a manager in a large company;
perhaps she has a t-square to Pluto in Leo in the seventh house, with Mars in Taurus in the fourth opposing
Mercury in Scorpio in the tenth. She wants to become
trained as a psychologist, but doesn't want to sacrifice her material security while procuring her degree.
She can compromise by taking a cut in pay and working
in the personnel department of the same company or she
can fulfill the needs of both her Taurus and Scorpio
by attending inexpensive Home Town University at nights
(rather than Prestige University 100 miles away) while
continuing in her present job. Her focal planet Pluto,
functioning in both seventh house Leo and first house
Aquarius (as she totally involves herself in her schooling, develops counselling skills and becomes friends
with other psychology students) will give her the resourcefulness and energy she needs to finish her degree; her focal planet is, essentially, the third point
of the triangle, "the controlling and regulating principle."

Woman 1

Woman 2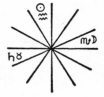

88

Consider another Taurus/Scorpio possibility. A woman has Moon in Scorpio in the seventh house in opposition to Saturn in Taurus in the first house, both forming a t-square to Sun in Aquarius in the tenth. She is torn between her desire for a secure and stable lifestyle and her desire for intense relationships. She could compromise, by entering into a loveless marriage with a rich philanderer and devoting herself to her career to escape from the anguish of his infidelity. Or, she may, while looking for a more satisfying relationship, develop a deep and enduring connection with an older friend at work, who eventually becomes her roommate. Here, not only are many (obviously not all) of her Saturn/Moon and Taurus/Scorpio needs satisfied, but the energy of her Aquarius Sun in the tenth house is integrated with empty Leo in the fourth house, because she has established a warm and satisfying relationship at home.

The focal planet is therefore a key to synthesizing a t-square. It can help you to become aware of new alternatives which will enable you to fulfill both sides of your opposition. But you can also begin with your opposition and attempt to integrate it. The expansion of consciousness which occurs as you transcend the conflicting polarities can awaken you to new expressions of your focal planet and release energy which it can use to direct the ongoing synthesis of the opposition.

You need to understand the planets, signs and houses in your opposition. You must consider each part, and its relation to the whole. By focusing upon the positive expression of each sign in your opposition, and allowing each to contribute to the highest expression of the other, you can begin to actualize the potential of your t-square configuration.

ARIES/LIBRA

Negative Expression

Your Aries/Libra opposition indicates that you seek a balanced lifestyle and harmonious relationships, but constantly upset your equilibrium by giving in to your equally strong desire for excitement. Your moods fluctuate from high to low and rarely stabilize at center; likewise you alternate between plunging impulsively into new and stimulating activities, and feeling paralyzed, able to evaluate a variety of alternatives but unable to commit yourself to one course of action.

Your insecurity about your own identity leads you to become overly involved in personal relationships, to look to other people for affirmation and approval, to be oversensitive to their reactions, and to try too hard to be liked. Often, you enter a new relationship with enthusiasm and ardor, only to discover that your intensity drives the other person away, or prevents the bonds between you from becoming firm and enduring. The energy which you invest into forming relationships demands release, and may lead you to overemphasize the sexual, allowing your passion and excitement to convince you that you and your partner are emotionally, intellectually and spiritually compatible.

Once you have formed a relationship in which you feel appreciated, your need to satisfy your desires and maintain your freedom asserts itself. Often, without being aware of it, you attempt to dominate your partner. By maintaining a charming, agreeable facade and cultivating pleasing behaviors, you discover that you get your way without having to make any significant compromises. Frequently, you define "50-50" in a relationship to your own advantage and become angry when you believe that the other person is not contributing equally or treating you fairly. Unwittingly then, you provoke the very conflict which you seek to avoid.

ARIES/LIBRA POLARITIES

ARIES	LIBRA
action-oriented	relationship-oriented
self-directed	dependent upon others
self-centered, self-assertive	striving for equality, justice and fairness
maintaining personal liberty, competing	cooperating, accommodating, developing committed and mutually satisfying relationships, law-abiding
pleasing self, satisfying own desires	pleasing others, attempting to be liked
frank, direct, outspoken	tactful, flattering
intense, energetic	poised, placid, lethargic, paralyzed
sexual, passionate	cultivating loving relationships
initiating, impulsive, quick	weighing alternatives, evaluating, delaying action, indecisive
subjective, aware of own point of view	objective, aware of all points of view
seeking excitement provoking conflict	striving for balance, peace and harmony, avoiding conflict, harmonizing, mediating

Aries/Libra Synthesis: Self-Direction in Relationship

The synthesis of your Aries/Libra opposition requires that Aries redirect the negative qualities of
Libra and that Libra moderate the negative qualities
of Aries.

Your Arian initiative enables you to conquer in-
decision, to select one course of action rather than
spin your wheels indefinitely while considering a variety of alternatives. Your sense of self and contact
with your needs and desires helps you to go after what
you want in life, to take the initiative, to act on
your own and to find pleasure in your activities, so
that you are not dependent upon other people for satisfaction. Able to bring a strong sense of your identity
into personal encounters, you enter in a relationship
as an independent individual, and are therefore able
to form relationships which promote your growth rather
than cater to your dependency and weakness. By maintaining your individuality, you encourage the individuality of others, and develop connections which are
firm and mutually liberating. Because you are aware of
your own needs, you are able to recognize, respond to,
and satisfy the needs of others.

Your Arian energy also motivates you to initiate
interpersonal contact and to enliven your relationships with your enthusiasm, sparkle and zest for life.
It enables you to enjoy social activities, and to
strengthen your bonds with others by involving yourselves together in activities (often cultural) which
are satisfying to each of you. Your directness leads
you to relate openly and personally, to assert your
needs and desires, and to spontaneously express affection and love. The passion so characteristic of Aries
translates your love into sexual expression and motivates you to actively please your partner as well as
yourself.

Because you are willing to deal with conflict,
you are able to confront the problems that arise between you and other people, and to invest the energy
necessary to resolve them; as a result, you gain the

confidence that you can tackle whatever future obstacles arise. Your relationships become characterized by mutual understanding and give-and-take, rather than superficial harmony. By being yourself and learning how to satisfy your own needs in cooperation with others, you discover that you don't have to cultivate a phony personality to win approval; you can be loved as you are.

Libra/Aries Synthesis: Balanced and Cooperative Action

The influence of Libra upon Arian excitability is moderating and balancing. Your Libran ability to perceive and evaluate alternatives before acting can help you to determine which of many possibilities is most viable, and can restrain you from hasty action. Able to experience the pull of conflicting choices, you can expand your consciousness and make decisions which fulfill your deepest self rather than discharge momentary impulses. Libra prevents you from overdoing and depleting your energy; it urges you to act in moderation, and when other people are involved, to demonstrate fairness, consideration and a willingness to cooperate.

Your Libran awareness of others and your desire for harmony inclines you to assert your Arian desires and feelings without antagonizing the other person, and to resolve interpersonal problems by discovering solutions which are of mutual benefit. Libra teaches you that you can compromise or cooperate and still retain your independence, and that you can engage in social activities and still satisfy your most urgent desires. Libra makes sure that your Arian self discovers that by knowing how to please other people and by remaining sensitive to their needs, you are fulfilled and that you incline them to respect your individuality and to want to please you.

The love that your Libran nature gives and receives strengthens your Arian sense of identity and enriches your sexual encounters. The laws you uphold and the commitments which you make to others liberate your energy, allowing you to experience increased

motivation and freedom of action. By following laws
and forming bonds which are in accordance with your
deepest inclinations, you become self-directed -
guided not by the many small selves within you which
would scatter you and separate you from other people,
but rather by the greater Self at the center of your
being, which teaches you to live by higher laws and to
form loving, enduring relationships.

TAURUS/SCORPIO

Negative Expression

Your Taurus/Scorpio opposition inclines you to be
overly preoccupied with satisfying your material and
physical desires and with indulging yourself in the
pleasures of the senses. Because you experience considerable inertia before taking action or asserting
yourself, you allow tension to build until it becomes
unbearable, and then erupt in a powerful and often destructive manner.

Your tendency first to wallow in and then give
free rein to your raging emotions erodes your self-
esteem and prevents you from relaxing and appreciating
the simple joys of life. Your low self esteem and im-
moderate appetites may result in unsatisfying and even
degrading sexual experiences which leave you feeling
hungry and even more at the mercy of your desires.
When not giving in to these desires, you sit in judgment upon yourself, berating yourself for feeling over-
powered by material or physical urges, rather than discovering ways to fulfill yourself or to sublimate your
frustrated energies.

In your relationships, you are strong-willed and
demanding. Because you do not feel in possession of
yourself or capable of functioning self-sufficiently,
you manipulate other people into conforming to your
will, while considering their efforts to satisfy their
needs as domination and stubbornly resisting their influence. You are most likely to experience interpersonal conflicts because of your inability to resolve

TAURUS/SCORPIO POLARITIES

TAURUS	SCORPIO
self-sufficient	merging emotionally and sexually, sharing material resources
developing your resources, earning a living	helping others develop their resources, using their resources
focusing upon the concrete or tangible	investigating, penetrating beneath the surface
practical, productive, concerned with concrete results	concerned with energy and its use, occult interests
seeking material security, materially indulgent	gaining power through use of the material
personal power	power over others
satisfying your needs and desires	demanding that others satisfy you, seeking mutual satisfaction
warm, devoted	healing, regenerating
desiring security in love, enjoying sensory pleasures	desiring sexual release, passionate
self esteem	self-conquering
accumulating material goods, enslaved by material/physical desires	eliminating inessentials, overcoming or sublimating desires
easygoing, inert, lazy	intense, transforming, experiencing death and rebirth

sexual or material issues, or because of your jealousy and possessiveness.

Taurus/Scorpio Synthesis: Constructive Power

The synthesis of your Taurus/Scorpio opposition requires that Taurus stabilize and channel the negative qualities of Scorpio and that Scorpio transform the negative qualities of Taurus.

Your Taurean preoccupation with values and productivity can enable you to value the psychic energy which is available to you, and to channel your inner turmoil into practical accomplishments. Taurus can give you the patience and stability necessary to concentrate that energy and to release it at an appropriate time and in an appropriate manner. The groundedness and self-possession of Taurus can aid you in confronting the dark forces within you; the self-esteem of Taurus can enable you to accept those forces as a valid part of you, to appreciate their constructive possibilities, and to expand your awareness of your inner resources. Such a strengthening of your foundations can further increase your self-worth and self-sufficiency as well as your resourcefulness in satisfying your desires; as a result, you can demand less of other people, and abandon controlling behaviors designed to force them to conform to your will.

Your Taurean sense of values and self-esteem can also lead you to form more satisfying sexual relationships. Your warmth and devotion allows you to relax and experience greater sexual fulfillment; your sensual nature inclines you to enjoy the pleasures of touching and to place less emphasis upon passion and its resulting climax. Finally, the patience so characteristic of Taurus can enable you to delay satisfaction until you are with the right partner, and both of you are in a frame of mind conducive to mutual enjoyment.

Taurus can also aid Scorpio by refusing to allow every experience to become a life-and-death matter, and by teaching you to appreciate what you have - the simple and stable joys of your life as well as the intense experiences of energy release and transformation.

Scorpio/Taurus Synthesis: Transformed Desire

Scorpio can transform the influence of Taurus in your chart by destroying your Taurean inertia and placidity, and urging you to direct your will toward satisfactions which are deeper than those of material pleasures and a hedonistic lifestyle. Penetrating to the very core of your psyche, Scorpio releases potent energy - energy which is capable of transforming matter and enabling you to function productively in the material world, and energy necessary to overcome material attachments and control insatiable appetites.

Scorpio enables you to satisfy desire, to conquer desire or to sublimate desire. Its penetrating insight allows you to experience yourself as more than your physical body and to confront energies and laws that transcend the material plane. Many of the goods which your Taurean self has accumulated may be eliminated by Scorpio, which forces you to refine and remake your value system so that you appreciate what is essential in your life and rid yourself of the baggage that characterizes a life of ease.

Scorpio can demand that you prevail over your Taurean self-indulgence but it may also lead you through sensuality to the heights of sexual experience. Scorpio adds depth and passion to Taurean warmth and devotion. In the right circumstances, it allows you to *merge* with another psychically as well as physically, and then to *emerge* with a firmer sense of self, having let go of yourself long enough to re-establish your connection to the greater energies from which all of us draw nourishment. The mystical quality of sexual union directs Taurean energies toward higher fulfillment; the satisfaction of physical release eliminates excess tension and contributes to your ability to function productively. When sublimated, Scorpionic energies can inspire you to artistic expression which is vital and powerful because it draws from the depths of the psyche.

Your Scorpionic sense of privacy can further promote Taurean self-containment and self-sufficiency, insuring that you do not divulge information which leaves you feeling overly vulnerable or in the power of another.

Both Taurus and Scorpio are strong-willed, determined and resourceful signs; together, they can lead to phenomenal accomplishment. Your Scorpio can help you to use your Taurean resources, and also the resources others have and willingly share, for mutual benefit. Your perceptiveness and your ability to deal with conflict (to confront the darker side of human nature and harness its energy for higher purposes) strengthen your self-esteem and build the self-esteem of other's, who learn to value you and themselves because of your regenerating influence.

GEMINI/SAGITTARIUS

Negative Expression

Your Gemini/Sagittarius opposition suggests that you scatter your energies, engaging in too many activities, pursuing a wide variety of intellectual interests or relating to a large number of people. Attempting to do everything, you restlessly flit from one path to another, often exhibiting careless behavior or involving yourself only superficially in each of your endeavors.

You are a mental person, but rarely allow your mind to focus upon one course of study long enough to develop any expertise. Frequently, you become carried away with theories or meaningless bits of data, attempting to gain control over your reality by logic, substituting knowledge for experience, or philosophizing endlessly about everyday existence without actually applying your understanding to the way you live your life. You tend to be either overly preoccupied

GEMINI/SAGITTARIUS POLARITIES

<u>GEMINI</u>	<u>SAGITTARIUS</u>
living in the present, focusing upon immediate realities	aware of the future, planning, gaining perspective
observant, making connections, responding to stimuli	assimilating, processing and conceptualizing one's perceptions
gaining information, collecting data, knowledgeable	developing understanding and wisdom, seeking meaning, enlightened
concerned with facts and figures, scientific, empirical, thinking inductively (particular to general)	concerned with attitudes and theories, philosophical, thinking deductively (general to particular)
logical, rational, emphasizing reason	transcending reason, open to revelation, religious
amoral, unconcerned with ethical implications	moral, concerned with principles and ethics
versatile, pursuing many unrelated interests, possessing many skills	purposeful, pursuing a meaningful direction
scattered, restless	overextended, carried away with an activity
interacting, associating with diverse people	reaching out, carried away with a relationship
communicating, enjoying daily conversations	teaching, guiding, engaging in philosophical discussions

with trivia, or lost in higher conceptual realms
which have little relationship to your daily circumstances.

A manipulator of words, you talk incessantly,
often playing intellectual word games with other
people or inundating them with a mass of irrelevant
or disconnected information. You purport to have all
the answers, but you often use your powers of reasoning and your repertoire of facts to support your bias-
es or to convince other people that you possess knowledge or understanding which you have not acquired.
Your struggle to verbalize your perceptions also interferes with your ability to form connections with
people on non-verbal levels, and to experience the
integration of mind, body and feeling which would enable you to contact and live by your own inner wisdom.

Gemini/Sagittarius Synthesis: Dissemination of Wisdom

The synthesis of your Gemini/Sagittarius opposition requires that Gemini apply and share the wisdom
of Sagittarius and that Sagittarius give purpose and
direction to the mental pursuits and immediate realities of Gemini.

Your Geminian restlessness, curiosity and need
for daily interaction leads you to make contact with
a variety of people who can help you to discover new
perspectives and gain new insights. Because Gemini is
articulate and enjoys communicating, you are able to
verbalize the understanding of Sagittarius and to involve yourself in inspirational discussions with
other people.

By focusing your attention upon your immediate
environment, Gemini insures that your Sagittarian wisdom is truly wisdom and can be applied to your daily
life; it prevents you from losing yourself in higher
realms which have no relationship or relevance to your
everyday circumstances. By submitting your attitudes
and beliefs to the Geminian tests of reality-facing
and logical thinking, you develop a conceptual system

100

or philosophy of life which is meaningful to you in
all situations and which helps you to progress along
your chosen path.

The reading, writing, reasoning and information-
gathering skills which your Geminian self masters, as
well as the rudimentary knowledge you acquire through
your schooling and your powers of perception, provides
you with a firm foundation, enabling you to further
your education and develop the intuitive and synthesizing capacities of your higher mind. Your diversity
of interests and eclectic mental pursuits incline
you to become multi-disciplinary; because you have a
vast reservoir of knowledge from which to draw as well
as the ability to make connections, your Sagittarian
nature is able to perceive the interrelationships between apparently unrelated bits of information and to
gain a wholistic perspective and an awareness of a
higher order which expands your consciousness and
deepens your faith.

Sagittarius/Gemini Synthesis: Inspired Reasoning

As Sagittarian inspiration and revelation illuminate your Geminian reasoning, you gain insights which
enrich your daily life. A new perspective, a consideration of the ethical implications of knowledge and
daily communication, and an awareness of the future
help you to function better in your personal routine.
Sagittarius directs your Geminian mind toward meaningful knowledge which furthers your development, expands your consciousness and enables you to perceive,
through the realms of higher understanding, a unity
of purpose which transcends the diversity of your experience.

By reaching out to other people with Sagittarian
enthusiasm and optimism, and by communicating your
understanding, you raise the level of your personal
interactions. You inspire, guide and uplift the people
around you, and draw to yourself new acquaintances and
activities which in turn stimulate you and satisfy
your Geminian quest for knowledge and diversity. But

Sagittarius does not allow you to scatter your energies too widely or to engage in conversations or interests which waste your mental, verbal and social capabilities. By revealing to you your life direction, Sagittarius provides you with a singleness of purpose; you are therefore able to make constructive daily choices and to experience the integration of self which enables you to think and communicate more effectively.

CANCER/CAPRICORN

Negative Expression

Your Cancer/Capricorn opposition indicates that you frequently feel emotionally deprived and undernourished. Because in your childhood you did not experience a healthy balance between nurturing warmth and wise discipline, you have difficulty satisfying your emotional needs while functioning as a mature and capable adult. On the one hand, you become excessively dependent upon other people and want them to take care of you; on the other hand, you make inordinate demands upon yourself to respond to other people's needs and to act self-sufficiently and responsibly at all times.

Because you cannot really help others or appreciate their caring when you yourself are perpetually dissatisfied, you become increasingly despondent and self-doubting. You withdraw into a shell, brooding and worrying incessantly, unable either to give or receive love. Or, you substitute security for emotional fulfillment by clinging to your family or devoting yourself totally to your career. Overly preoccupied with your role as parent, you may try unsuccessfully to satisfy your needs through your children.

Attempting to meet all your needs through dependent love or compulsive work is no solution to your dilemma. Your moodiness and dissatisfaction prevent you from concentrating and applying yourself to the

CANCER/CAPRICORN POLARITIES

CANCER	CAPRICORN
moody, emotionally unstable, fluid	controlled, closed, emotionally inhibited, self-disciplined
sensitive, vulnerable	insensitive, cold, stoic
empathetic, sympathetic, responsive	detached, isolated, unresponsive
mothering, nurturing, protecting, pampering, smothering	fathering, setting limits, controlling, exercising power and authority
attached, dependent	self-sufficient
passive, timid, retreating	industrious, determined
psychic, intuitive, attuned to the unconscious	grounded, highly conscious, attuned to external realities
developing roots, seeking personal nourishment	success-oriented, ambitious, seeking public recognition
concerned with the personal and domestic, family or home-oriented, desiring family security	concerned with the professional and material, desiring professional security

job at hand; your dependency upon your family weakens
you and leads you to feel increasingly inadequate.
The more negative you become, the less effectively
you function; the less effectively you function, the
more negative you become.

Cancer/Capricorn Synthesis: Nourishing Discipline

The synthesis of your Cancer/Capricorn opposition
requires that Cancer lend its nurturing sensitivity
to Capricornian discipline and labor, and that Capricorn apply its self-control and self-sufficiency to
Cancerian feeling.

Your Cancerian attunement to your emotions enables you to experience and channel feelings which
interfere with your work and responsibilities. Cancer
teaches you that by attending to your emotional needs
and learning to nourish yourself, you not only become
more fulfilled, but you also become stronger and increasingly self-sufficient, able to cope with the restrictions or deprivations which Capricorn may demand
that you experience.

The emotional nourishment which Cancer seeks and
provides inclines you to form rich and enduring connections with other people. You are able to commit
yourself and remain loyal not only because of your
sense of responsibility, but also because you are
willing to deal with the vulnerabilities and insecurities of personal relationships and because you know
the emotional depth and satisfaction that you can experience with another person. Because you are aware
of your own sensitivity and can deal with your ever-
changing moods, you are responsive and empathetic
with others, inclining them to take you seriously and
to, in turn, commit themselves to you.

Your contact with the vast reservoir of your Cancerian unconscious also enables you to remain in
touch with the "child" within you and to age grace-
fully. It helps you to be an effective parent, able
to respond to your children's needs because you can

cope with your own, and able to temper your discipline with love. Because your behavior is nurturing as well as firm, your children respect your authority and willingly become self-disciplined and reliable. The warm family life which you provide and experience gives you and them a solid foundation which encourages each of you to function more maturely and responsibly in the outside world.

The satisfactions which you experience in your personal life enhance your professional life. Because you are not driven to substitute success for emotional deprivation, you can relax and work more effectively; you can enjoy the process of work as well as the recognition you achieve. Cancer helps you to choose a profession which nourishes your inner self and which, as a result, spurs you to function at your best. It allows you to become emotionally involved in your work and to experience its satisfactions, as well as to relate personally and sensitively to the public so that you earn their good will. It may even incline you to choose a domestic or helping profession in which you fulfill your emotional needs while enriching the personal lives of other people.

Capricorn/Cancer Synthesis: Stabilized Emotions

Your Capricornian self-sufficiency helps you to cope with emotional conflicts and to fulfill your own needs; your self-control enables you to stabilize your emotions and prevent them from overwhelming you. Because you are willing to take responsibility for your actions, you are able to confront childish behaviors, bad habits and feelings of helplessness, and to rid of those past patterns which are no longer nourishing.

Capricorn filters your experience, protecting you from indulging in debilitating emotions and from absorbing too easily the psychological confusions of the people around you. Because your sense of your own boundaries does not allow you to lose yourself in other people's suffering, you do not become overly upset by their problems, and you respond wisely and maturely, offering Cancerian support but also encouraging their strength and refusing to feed their weakness. As a result, Capricorn contributes to your emotional well-being and to the well-being of the people around you.

This awareness of limits and the determination to function in an adult manner help you to be a responsible and effective parent, nurturing your children but also enforcing discipline. As they develop their self-control and become more self-reliant, your home life improves and you become more secure in your knowledge that you have raised a healthy family. Your Capricornian responsibility enables you to make firm commitments to family and loved ones, enduring difficult times and working diligently, when necessary, to provide for them. Because you will, at times, deprive yourself for the sake of your family, you experience, at other times, the emotional rewards of having the family security and love that is so important to you.

Capricorn teaches you to channel your emotional energy into fulfilling work. Your productivity and sense of accomplishment also improve your home life, insuring that you do not smother the people around you by regarding them as your only source of satisfaction. Capricorn may help you to translate your domestic and personal interests into professional capabilities, orienting you to work in the home or to function successfully in a domestic or nurturing occupation.

LEO/AQUARIUS

Negative expression:

Your Leo/Aquarius opposition indicates that you confuse your own will with the greater Will that directs humanity. You seek the truth, but too often allow your ego to convince you that you are the only voice of truth, and that your dictates should be

LEO/AQUARIUS POLARITIES

LEO	AQUARIUS
self-expressive, creative, playful	intellectual, abstract, inventive
warm, radiant, romantic	friendly to all, brotherly
personal, emotional, spontaneous	impersonal, detached, unemotional
loyal, faithful	freedom-loving, unattached
generous, giving	humanitarian, liberal
possessing firm sense of identity, self-centered, egotistical, proud	political, identifies with humanity, group or social cause
individualistic	nonconformist, rebellious
attention-seeking, commanding, bossy, wanting to rise above the group	group-oriented, promoting equality, cooperative, tolerant
self-seeking, attuned to personal desires	truth-seeking, attuned to universal laws

followed. Through your interpretations of universal laws and your intellectualizations of your erratic behavior, you self-righteously force your way upon other people, while attempting to persuade them that you are a uniquely dedicated and selfless human being.

Your espousal of humanitarian ideals leads you to become active in a group or cause in which you believe, but you are unable to live by your ideals in your personal life; you claim to love humanity, but do not know how to relate to individuals in a truly loving manner. Frequently, you lose yourself in high-sounding abstractions or become involved with group activities that prevent you from forming close relationships.

In any group, you seek to fulfill your ego needs by attaining a position of power in which you can act freely, and by using that power to impose your desires upon others, under the guise of good will or enlightened reason. You preach democracy, but establish an autocracy in which you are sole dictator. From the heights, you project Leonian warmth and heartfelt generosity, but you usually turn on the light inside of you only to win the attention and appreciation of your public.

You resist domination, but dominate others. With your children, you use the ploy of friendship to compel them to submit to you. In other relationships, you maintain control by cultivating a crowd of faithful admirers rather than establishing equal and mutually satisfying friendships. In romance, often mistaking friendship for love, you demand affection and loyalty, but are unable either to be a friend or to express love without wielding power over your partner.

Leo/Aquarius Synthesis: Loving Humanitarianism

The synthesis of your Leo/Aquarius opposition requires that Leo contribute its loving warmth and self-confident leadership to Aquarian detachment and intellectuality, and that Aquarius apply its universalism and humanitarianism to Leonian egocentricity and pride.

Your Leonian sense of self enables you to be a self-directed individualist, aware of the freedom that results from following the laws of your inner being, rather than rebelling against society. Because of your sturdy ego, you are able to cope with the inevitable changes that Aquarius brings to your life, whether self-imposed or resulting from external circumstances.

Your Leonian capacity to open your heart to the people around you, to relate personally and give generously from your own abundance, enriches your friendships and inspires you to live, not merely preach, your humanitarianism. The warmth which you experience and project expresses your Aquarian love for mankind; your self-possession and self-rule contribute to the establishment of a true democracy, in which people rule themselves rather than, feeling powerless, seek to dominate or be dominated.

The groups to which you belong are enlivened by your Leonian presence; your enthusiasm and playful spirit help others to relax and enjoy their activities. Because of your confidence and leadership, you give power to a group and help it to become a cohesive entity, capable of fulfilling its social purpose. Your personal involvement in social causes inspires others to involve themselves and to experience the fulfillment of actualizing Aquarian ideals.

Through fully experiencing the personal, Leo taps realms of the collective unconscious and perceives the universal truths of Aquarius. Such knowledge, acquired and communicated on a human rather than abstract level, is alive, not sterile. By also experiencing the universal feelings that reside deep within the personal, you identify with all humanity and live the Aquarian ideals of openmindedness, tolerance and brotherhood. Your awareness of your own ego needs helps you to differentiate your small will from the greater Will; your contact with your center of light enables you to draw sustenance from the light which illuminates all humanity, and to help other people become aware of the light which shines through them.

The independent spirit of your Aquarian self helps Leo become less dependent upon the applause of the public and more self-directed. Your Aquarian ability to identify with humanity and perceive universal levels of consciousness enables your Leonian ego to transcend its narrow boundaries. Because Aquarius attunes you to universal laws, you are able to discover and live by the laws of your own nature which benefit both yourself and mankind. Because your will is aligned with the greater Will, you experience increased confidence and personal fulfillment.

Your Aquarian concern for humanity also inclines you to radiate the love and light within you so that you illuminate everyone with whom you come in contact, rather than merely a small circle of admirers. Because you understand the importance of friendships which are equal and mutually satisfying, you do not need to establish relationships in which you always play king or queen to your devoted followers; you are capable of being a true friend and giving love even when you do not receive a highly appreciative response.

Aquarius provides a channel for your Leonian self-expression, enabling you to contribute creatively to friendships, groups and social causes, expressing yourself personally while simultaneously directing your energies toward a purpose which extends beyond yourself.

VIRGO/PISCES

Negative expression:

Your Virgo/Pisces opposition indicates that you are a perfectionist, enamored with the ideal and perpetually dissatisfied with the realities of your life. Easily disillusioned, you retreat into fantasy or drift aimlessly, paralyzed by the confusion you have created. Either you become stuck attempting to resolve one particular issue and lose perspective, or you experience the whole situation and its resolution, but

VIRGO/PISCES POLARITIES

<u>VIRGO</u>	<u>PISCES</u>
analytical, mental	intuitive, imaginative, highly sensitive
particular, concerned with details, exacting	perceiving the whole, synthesizing
discriminating, critical	undiscriminating, accepting
organized, orderly, systematic, efficient, industrious	disorganized, chaotic, confused, careless
anxious, worried, concerned	flowing, surrendering, avoiding
concerned with everyday realities, practical	otherworldly, escapist, impractical, spiritual, transcendent
perfectionistic	idealistic
self-doubting, negative, dissatisfied	self-pitying, cynical, disillusioned, oversensitive
helpful, serving, useful	compassionate, devoted, responsive, tender
modest, unassuming	self-sacrificing, easily victimized, selfless
health-conscious, hypochondriacal	prone to psychosomatic disorders or addictions, physically sensitive

unwisely trust that it will take care of itself, and
fail to apply yourself to the tasks that are required
of you. Frequently, you escape from work or other responsibilities which seem mundane or tedious, and then
become lost in a fog of details when you are forced
to confront all that you have avoided. Your emotional
self-indulgence prevents you from thinking clearly;
your mind meanders from irrelevancy to irrelevancy,
focusing upon peripheral items rather than issues of
primary concern.

Because you are emotionally insecure and cannot
adequately cope with your daily responsibilities, you
turn inward, and give in to self-pity and negative
thinking. Your emotional sensitivity may affect your
health, leading you to experience psychosomatic disorders or paralysis, or to become addicted to drugs,
tobacco or alcohol.

In relationships, you attempt to compensate for
a weak self-image by meekly submitting to the needs
of others. Espousing ideals of sacrifice and service,
you allow yourself to be exploited and then feel victimized. You exercise little discrimination when entering into relationships, idealizing the potential
of the other person rather than viewing him or her
realistically. At first, you are overly accepting and
responsive; then, when you confront reality, you become disillusioned and bitter, critical of the person
in whom you had so deeply believed and even more negative and insecure about yourself.

Virgo/Pisces Synthesis: Discriminating Sensitivity

The synthesis of your Virgo/Pisces opposition requires that Virgo apply its mental keenness and discrimination to Piscean confusion and submissiveness
and that Pisces lend its spiritual sensitivity and
acceptance to Virgoan analysis and criticism.

Your Virgoan ability to analyze your perceptions
and intuitions insures that you can bring order and
clarity to your emotional confusion, rather than allow yourself to drown in a whirlpool of feeling. In-

stead of blindly trusting each person or circumstance in your life, you assess each one realistically, carefully selecting relationships and activities which uplift you and enable you to reach Piscean heights of inspiration and transcendence. Virgo helps you to determine which current will carry you to which shore, so that you surrender only to that current which accords with your inner vision, which has practical application, and which enables you to fulfill your highest ideals.

Virgo teaches you to translate your compassion and spirituality into service, applying yourself with dedication to even the most menial tasks, provided that they benefit you and others. Encouraging your Piscean self to make a useful contribution to humanity, Virgo directs you toward a social service or health occupation; it also disciplines your imagination, enabling you to channel your inspiration into creative work, and to develop expertise as an artist, writer or musician.

Your Virgoan preoccupation with perfection leads you to perfect yourself so that you are more capable of living by your ideals. Virgo helps you to care for your emotional well-being by filtering out emotions which poison or debilitate you; it directs you to care for your physical well-being so that you experience the healthy flow of energy which awakens your Piscean self to inspiration and love.

Because you care for yourself, you are discriminating in your relationships and protect yourself from people who would harm or exploit you. Pisces urges you to give emotionally, but Virgo insures that you give to the right people in the right circumstances, and that your giving does not weaken you and others, but strengthens you both and opens you even more fully to the divine energies within.

Pisces/Virgo Synthesis: Compassionate Service

Your Piscean attunement to cosmic energies inspires your thinking, enabling you to view the details of your

existence in terms of the whole, and therefore to de-
vote yourself to each of your daily tasks. Your spirituality illumines every facet of your life. By letting
go and flowing with the energies of the universe, you
rest your mind and are able to think more clearly; you
also contact your intuition, which helps you to focus
upon the essentials of your life and to avoid the endless intellectualizing which results from analyzing an
issue without listening to your inner voice. By using
your imagination to create positive thought forms, you
not only prevent your Virgoan self from wallowing in
negative thinking, but you also develop constructive
attitudes which help you to function more efficiently.

The inner vision of Pisces guides you to choose
work which is personally meaningful, usually because
it allows you to be of service or to express yourself
creatively. Because your work is emotionally satisfying, you are motivated to apply yourself. Because you
can flow with the demands of your daily routine, you
do not poison yourself with worry or anxiety; you are
able to relax and fulfill your responsibilities. Your
Piscean sensitivity contributes to your ability to
work with other people, because you can empathize with
their feelings and respond compassionately to their
problems.

Pisces teaches you that work performed with love
is a far greater service and far more uplifting than
work devoid of feeling and purpose. In your personal
relationships, it reveals to you the power of acceptance, which softens criticism and renders the other
person more willing to listen to your point of view.
By enabling you to accept yourself, to hear and to re-
vere the voice of the divine within you, Pisces directs you to care for yourself, to treat yourself tenderly, and to look after your emotional and physical
well-being. Virgo is concerned with health; Pisces
prevents ill health by opening your mind and body to
the healing energies of compassion and love.

OPPOSING HOUSES

The opposing houses in your t-square, as well as the opposing signs, indicate polarities in your life which need to be balanced or synthesized. Because you are torn in two directions between the opposing houses of your opposition, you need to develop ways to express both areas of your life - either by allowing yourself to focus upon each house in turn without losing awareness of the other, or by developing ways to fulfill the needs of both houses simultaneously.

This chapter, like the chapter on sign polarities, is concerned with understanding the nature of your t-square opposition, and with considering a variety of possibilities for synthesizing and integrating its separate realms. It is likewise concerned with understanding the nature of the imbalance between the house of your focal planet and the house of your empty space. Only by understanding the areas of life which you overemphasize and those which you ignore can you begin to cultivate a balance between the focal and empty houses as well as the opposing houses. Since you are not likely to have a planet positioned in the empty house of your t-square, you should interpret the empty house according to the sign and ruler of the empty degree; if the sign and ruler on the cusp are different, the meanings of these should also be taken into consideration.

Whether or not you have a t-square, this chapter can be helpful to you in clarifying the meaning of any oppositions in your chart, and in discovering ways to resolve the imbalance of the opposing houses.

The houses which follow are arranged by polarities, with each area of life denoted by the house contrasted, when possible, with an area of life denoted by the opposing house. In many cases, the meanings given are similar to the meanings of the signs which rule the houses in the natural zodiac; likewise, the synthesis of the houses has much in common with the synthesis of the corresponding signs. The ideas for synthesis which follow each discussion of house polarities combine most, if not all, of the contrasting expressions of the house. Only a few may be relevant to you, because the signs and planets associated with a given house in your chart, and the context of your life, may incline you to focus upon only a few of the expressions of each house; however, those few which may be relevant can aid you in discovering ways to resolve the dilemma of your opposing houses.

The polarity indicated in your chart between the focal planet and the empty space must also be resolved. The house of the focal planet and the house of the empty space will always be in opposition. In some cases, as when your focal planet is within the last five degrees of a house, its influence may extend to the next house; you would, therefore, want to consult the meaning of the next house and understand its polarity. Frequently, however, the opposition in your t-square, or other oppositions in your chart, may occur between houses which lie five rather than six houses apart. A planet may be positioned four degrees before the end of the second house, and oppose, with a five degree orb, a planet one degree into the ninth house. In this situation, the polarity of the third and ninth houses should be considered to be the most important polarity, since a planet's influence upon a house is at its peak near the end of the cusp. The planet in question, near the end of the second house, would have a combined second house/third house influence.

If you have such an opposition in your chart, you can benefit not only by studying the polarities described here, and the corresponding ideas for synthesis, but also by contrasting the meanings of the houses which are not directly in opposition, and by attempting

116

HOUSE POLARITIES IN THE T-SQUARE

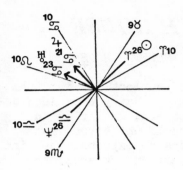

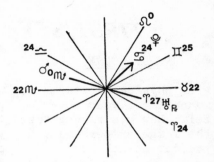

Here, the opposing planets, Sun and Neptune, are clearly in opposing succedent houses. The focal planets, Jupiter and Uranus, are also in a succedent house. The house polarities which need to be integrated are the 2nd and 8th, and the 11th and 5th.

Here, the opposing planets, Mars and Uranus, are clearly in opposing cadent houses. However, the focal planet, Pluto, is in a succedent house. The house polarities which need to be integrated are the 6th and 12th, and the 8th and 2nd.

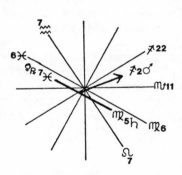

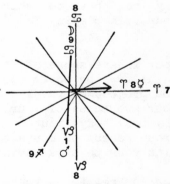

Here, the opposing planets, Venus and Saturn, are located near the cusps of succedent and cadent houses. The focal planet, Mars, is in an angular house. Both the 5th and 11th and the 6th and 12th houses need to be integrated in addition to the polarity of the 1st and 7th houses.

Here, the opposing planets, Moon and Mars, are not located in opposing houses; Moon is in an angular house. A polarity is created between the 3rd and 10th houses, which must be understood and integrated. The 1st and 7th house polarities must also be integrated.

on your own to find a balance between them or to discover ways in which you can integrate and synthesize
their diverse meanings.

FIRST/SEVENTH HOUSE

FIRST HOUSE

your physical appearance;
mannerisms; your outer
self; how others see you;
the image or persona you
present to others

your awareness of your
physical appearance and
outer image; the facets
of yourself that dominate
your awareness; your
self-consciousness; your
desire to control the
way you appear to others;
your role-playing

your innate sense of
identity; the power that
you project outwardly;
your awareness of your
physical body; your
groundedness or contact
with your physical being

how you relate to your-
self; the harmony or
discord you experience
with yourself

SEVENTH HOUSE

what you look for in other
people; what you project onto others; qualities in
yourself which you want
others to express; the kind
of partner you seek; the
people you attract

your awareness of others;
your tendency to focus upon
personal relationships, particularly marriage or love
relationships; your tendency to lose yourself in
others; the kinds of relationships you form; how you
selectively choose or shape
these relationships

your awareness of other
people as separate individuals; how you make contact
with and react to other
people; how you relate on a
one-to-one basis

your ability to cooperate
with other people; the harmony or discord you experience in your relationships;
your marriages, business
partnerships, consulting relationships and other committed one-to-one relation-

	ships; dissolution of bonds, separation or divorce
your need to be physically (as well as mentally and emotionally) active; your go-getter tendencies	your need to relate on a one-to-one basis; your desire for committed personal relationships
your earliest years of life	your marriage years
your personal aspirations	the aspirations of your partner

HOW CAN YOU INTEGRATE YOUR FIRST AND SEVENTH HOUSES?

1. *Through your relationships, you can increase your awareness of the self you are projecting to others, gaining feedback which can help you to bring your outer and inner self into harmony.*

2. *You can form relationships with people who accept you and freely allow you to be yourself, or who share with you similar aspirations, desires and activities.*

3. *In contact with yourself and able to actively fulfill your own desires, you can understand the needs that other people have to remain in touch with themselves and to actively express and satisfy themselves in their own way. You can encourage them to be themselves.*

4. *In contact with yourself and grounded in your physical body, you can make total contact with other people without losing yourself. You can remain in touch with your own power and keep from giving your power away to others.*

5. *You can own the parts of yourself that you project rather than look outward to other people to express them for you. As a result, you can break free of*

119

compulsive tendencies to form relationships which
follow the same pattern and manifest the same prob-
lems.

6. By allowing yourself to become fully interested in
other people and to make total contact with them,
you can become less self-conscious and less con-
cerned with how others perceive you. You can drop
your role-playing and enter into truly "I-Thou"
relationships.

SECOND/EIGHTH HOUSE

SECOND HOUSE	EIGHTH HOUSE
how you earn your income; your earning capacity; fluctuations in personal income	your desire and capacity to receive money from outside sources such as marriage partner, investments, inheritance, trust funds, grants, taxes, insurance, business opportunities
your attitudes and actions in regard to budgeting and spending personal income; what you buy	your attitudes and actions in regard to budgeting, dividing, controlling and investing other people's income or shared income
your need to insure your own financial security by developing your earning power; your willingness to work diligently in order to increase your income	your need to insure your financial security by increasing your income from outside sources; your willingness to depend upon outside income sources
the extent to which you identify with and need to accumulate material possessions; how you use and care for your possessions	the importance to you of other people's possessions or shared possessions; how you use and care for other people's possessions

your self-worth; what you value in yourself

how you contribute to other people's self-worth; what you value in others

your ability to satisfy your own needs

your ability to respond to (and physically intuit) the needs of others

your psychological and physical resources and how you use them

the psychological and physical resources you help other people use and develop

your desire to be emotionally as well as financially self-sufficient

your desire to merge with others, to be emotionally as well as financially interdependent

what you believe that you deserve; what you owe yourself

what you believe others deserve; your obligations and debts

your attitudes toward sensual (as distinct from sexual) experience

your attitudes toward sexual experience; what you value about sex

your openness to your physical (as distinct from sexual) and material needs

your openness to core emotional, psychic and sexual energies and needs

your concern with survival and subsistence issues

your concern with death and rebirth, both physical and psychological; the role of death in your life

your tendencies to become absorbed with the practical, often surface issues of daily life

your desire to investigate sub-surface phenomena: psychology, the occult, physics and other energy-related realms

your need to develop a stable and secure base

your need to remain in touch with your own psy-

for yourself in the mate-
rial world

chological and sexual
energies and the energies
of the universe

your desire for exper-
iences which contribute
to your self-worth and
self-sufficiency

your desire for intense
experiences which trans-
form and regenerate you

HOW CAN YOU INTEGRATE YOUR SECOND AND EIGHTH HOUSES?

1. *You cultivate your abilities to help other people satisfy their own emotional/physical/material needs, or to develop their own emotional/physical/material resources.*

2. *You can earn a living by using these abilities. Depending upon the element, sign and planets in your eighth house, you may choose such occupations as accountant, psychologist, banker, editor, coach or doctor.*

3. *You can develop your eighth house abilities to investigate material, physical, psychological and occult energies. You may earn a living utilizing these skills, as a detective, researcher, psychic, astrologer, physicist, economist or fundraiser.*

4. *You can develop your self-esteem by valuing and giving yourself credit for these abilities.*

5. *You can, by consciously building your self esteem, overcome fears of losing yourself in others. You can allow yourself to become more emotionally and sexually open and more willing to acknowledge and experience your interdependence with others.*

6. *You can let go of your narrow definitions of self-sufficiency and learn to operate self-sufficiently in some realms of life, while experiencing and accepting your interdependence in other realms.*

7. *You can allow yourself to use the emotional/physi-*

cal/material resources which others freely give you in order to develop your own resources.

8. You can spend your money on books, courses, etc., which help you to come to terms with your own eighth house issues - issues of human relations, sexuality, occult understanding, medicine, economics, physics.

9. You can open yourself to experiences of a psychic, sexual or emotional nature which transform your awareness of your relationship to the universe, which help you to come to terms with death, and which enable you to function in the material world without defining yourself solely in terms of your material accomplishments and possessions.

THIRD/NINTH HOUSE

THIRD HOUSE	NINTH HOUSE
your response to your immediate environment; your concern with immediate issues; how you deal with everyday circumstances	your response to the ethical or future implications of immediate issues; your orientation toward the future
your need for variety, interaction and communication in daily life; your need to be on the move	your need for meaningful or purposeful activity; your desire to explore new or distant realms
your desire for short trips or vacations; the nature of your short trips	your desire for long distance travel; how you prefer to travel; foreign environments which appeal to you
your interaction with your neighbors and daily acquaintances	your connections with foreigners; long-distance connections

your relationships with brothers, sisters and other relatives

your relationships with grandchildren and in-laws

your communication-related activities - speechmaking, writing, printing, involvement with newspapers or other media

your publishing-related activities; your opportunities for publication

your involvement in your early education; early educational interests

your involvement in your higher education; your course of study in college

your concern with facts, specifics, concrete realities

your concern with abstractions, generalities, philosophical/ethical issues

your powers of perception; your awareness of your environment

your powers of understanding; your belief system, faith or philosophy of life

your desire for practical or concrete knowledge; your curiosity about your environment

your desire for philosophical or religious understanding and wisdom; your curiosity about distant realms

your development of practical skills, such as driving, sewing, typing or basic repairs

your quest for meaning; your search for answers

your practical, daily problem solving

ethical/legal matters you must resolve in higher courts

HOW CAN YOU INTEGRATE YOUR THIRD AND NINTH HOUSES?

1. You can apply your philosophical/religious/ethical

beliefs to your daily life, living by them rather than merely by theorizing about them.

2. You can develop practical skills or study areas of basic knowledge which are meaningful to you because they will enable you to eventually pursue a higher education, or because they will help you to fulfill your purpose in life.

3. You can ground your philosophical/religious ideas by developing related factual knowledge. You can develop your factual expertise on foreign affairs.

4. You can pursue an advanced degree in a practical field, such as printing, auto mechanics, journalism or media.

5. You can teach basic, practical courses in a college, or introduce philosophical/religious courses to a high school day or evening program. You can teach English to foreigners, either at home or abroad.

6. You can take a brief vacation to a foreign country, or an extended trip which allows you to interact with the people and participate in their daily life. By corresponding with foreigners, you can learn about their country and lifestyle.

7. You can take periodic short trips to educational or religious environments where you can study, teach or lecture. Religious retreats, personal growth weekends or educational conferences may refresh and inspire you.

8. You can help your brothers, sisters, other relatives or neighbors deal with their philosophical/ethical/educational issues, or spend your time with them travelling in a foreign country. If you have in-laws or grandchildren, you may want to take short trips with them, help them gain practical knowledge or skills, or aid them in coping with their daily lives.

9. *You can interact frequently with people with whom you can discuss philosophical or religious issues of concern to you, or your educational and travel interests. You may want to write about these interests, and publish your writings or share them with the people in your life.*

FOURTH/TENTH HOUSE

FOURTH HOUSE	TENTH HOUSE
the role of your mother or most nurturing parent in your life	the role of your father or most public parent in your life
your attunement to your inner self, to the roots of your being; your need to retreat within yourself or your family; the foundation you build within yourself or in your private life	your attunement to the public and to the outer world; your concern with public image, reputation and prestige; the foundation you build for yourself within society
your domestic orientation and interests; your interest in houses, land and your physical environment	your public or professional orientation and interests
your desire for a home and family; your willingness to become rooted within a family or communal network; your need to belong	your ambition in terms of career; your desire for success, fame or power; your desire to be self-employed or to be your own boss
the nature of your home and living situation or family life (both as a child and as an adult)	the nature of your profession

126

how you function at home or with family or roommates; the self you express at home; your relationship to your family	your relationship to the public or to your employer; the self you express or the roles you play with the public or your employer
your potential for satisfaction in your personal life	your potential for professional achievement
your interest in the past; your tendency to hold onto your past, particularly your childhood	your sense of direction in regard to society; your desire to break free of childhood and carve a niche for yourself in the world

HOW CAN YOU INTEGRATE YOUR FOURTH AND TENTH HOUSES?

1. *You can choose a profession which allows you to work in your home or in a domestic setting.*

2. *You can choose a profession which does not threaten your home and family life by requiring you to work long hours, to make frequent business trips, or to move from city to city.*

3. *You can choose a profession which involves domestic work or which is concerned with houses, land or family issues.*

4. *By entering the family profession, you can work toward your career goals with family support. Or, you can gain the support of your family members by sharing your professional interests and activities with them, by letting them help you with your work, and by showing them how your professional success can benefit them as well as yourself. You can also help them determine or fulfill their professional goals.*

5. *You can develop a professional "family", a group of people involved in the same field as you, with whom*

127

you can share both your personal and professional concerns.

6. *By drawing from the depths of yourself, by involving yourself emotionally in your work, and by expressing your personal/human self as well as your formal/business self with the public, you can increase your satisfaction in your work as well as your potential for success.*

7. *You can channel some of your ambition and drive to your family, understanding the important contribution you make to society by caring for their well-being. By working to establish a healthy and happy family network, you can experience pride and success in your private life, and enjoy the recognition you receive from those who have not been able to establish so satisfying a home life.*

FIFTH/ELEVENTH HOUSE

FIFTH HOUSE

your need for leisure or play time; your ability to relax or play

how you spend your leisure time; the games, hobbies and personal pleasures which appeal to you

your desire to express yourself creatively

the nature of your creative activities; how you express your creative energies

ELEVENTH HOUSE

your need to belong to a group or organization; your ability to function in a group

how you spend your time in groups or organizations

your desire to commit yourself to a social cause; your desire to reform society

the nature of your humanitarian activities; how you express your humanitarian inclinations

your romantic nature;
your desire for love
affairs

your orientation toward
friendship; your desire
for friendship

what you want from ro-
mance; the kinds of ro-
mantic relationships
which you seek; the
nature of your roman-
tic partners

what you want from friendship; the kinds of friendships you form; the kinds
of friends you choose

your desire for children;
the role children play in
your life; how you relate
to children

the role stepchildren, or
adopted children or other
people's children play in
your life; how you relate
to them

your own children, par-
ticularly your first
child

your stepchildren or adopted children

your willingness to
gamble or take risks;
your speculation and
adventure-seeking acti-
vities

your goals and objectives;
how goal-directed you are;
how you fulfill your goals

HOW CAN YOU INTEGRATE YOUR FIFTH AND ELEVENTH HOUSES?

1. *You can cultivate friendships with people who
   share similar creative interests and similar leisure time activities.*

2. *You and your friends can develop goals for yourselves in regard to your own creative projects, and
   can encourage each other to fulfill these goals.*

3. *You can involve yourself in creative projects which
   have a social significance and which you can contribute to the groups or organizations to which you
   belong or the causes in which you believe. You can
   make creative gifts for your friends.*

4. *You can join organizations or groups concerned with*

the creative arts.

5. *You can involve your children in your organizational activities.*

6. *You can spend time with your friends, their children and your children, engaging in activities which are enjoyable to people of all ages.*

7. *You can cultivate friends of the opposite sex, and enter into romantic relationships with people who are friends as well as lovers. You can attempt to remain friends with previous lovers.*

8. *You can meet potential romantic partners through humanitarian or social organizations in which you believe, choosing lovers with whom you share a common social purpose or commitment.*

9. *You and your lover can spend time together with friends, and can cultivate new friendships with people whose company you both enjoy.*

10. *You can become more willing to take emotional risks in your friendships.*

SIXTH/TWELFTH HOUSE

SIXTH HOUSE	*TWELFTH HOUSE*
your desire to be of service or of use through your job or daily routine	your desire to be of service to the needy – the ill, the disturbed, the imprisoned or handicapped; your compassion for people in need
the importance of work in your life; your ability to handle details efficiently; your organ-	the importance to you of an inner life; your ability to tap your own wellspring of inspiration or

izational abilities	transcendent faith; your ability to surrender to your unconscious
how you express yourself through your work or daily responsibilities	what you repress, avoid expressing or express indirectly; your hidden weaknesses and hidden strengths
your work environment; the structure of your working day	your need to work or function quietly behind the scenes
your desire to relate to co-workers or employees; your relationships with co-workers or employees	your need to relate to yourself; your need for solitude; your private self
your attitude toward health; your physical health	your psychological health; your psychological sensitivity; psychosomatic illnesses

HOW CAN YOU INTEGRATE YOUR SIXTH AND TWELFTH HOUSES?

1. *You can choose an occupation which makes few demands upon you, allowing you the privacy and time to yourself which you need.*

2. *You can develop sensitive, compassionate relationships with your co-workers, sharing with them your inner life and helping them with theirs.*

3. *You can choose a social service occupation which enables you to help the underprivileged, handicapped, disturbed, ill or imprisoned cope with their problems.*

4. *You can work in an institution such as a prison or hospital, handling the daily paperwork or organizing the schedule of daily activities.*

131

5. *You can choose work which involves you in the kinds of activities you might normally do alone in your spare time, or which otherwise nourishes your inner life.*

6. *Apart from your job, you might volunteer your services to institutions which may need your secretarial or administrative skills.*

7. *You can maintain your physical and emotional health by understanding your mind-body relationship, by caring for your body through proper diet and exercise, and caring for your mind by allowing yourself periods of mental stillness and cultivating a positive attitude. By engaging in such mind/body activities as yoga, t'ai chi, bioenergetics or muscular therapy, you can take care of yourself and become more capable of providing meaningful services to others.*

8. *You can, with appropriate training, become a psychotherapist or doctor, concerned not with either mind or body, but with the interplay of both. You can become a healer or a wholistic health practitioner.*

9. *By confronting and "working" on your psychological problems and bringing clarity and organization to your thinking, you can overcome your own inhibitions and fears.*

10. *You can deepen your own inner life through meditation, visualization and various spiritual practices as well as through experiences of creative inspiration. At peace with yourself and attuned to cosmic energies, you can be of service to humanity by simply being and radiating your inner light.*

INFLUENCES: TRANSITS, PROGRESSIONS, SYNASTRY

Your t-square is a dynamic configuration; it is constantly changing. Transits (including eclipses and lunations), progressions and solar return charts, as well as the aspects made by the planets of important people in your life, all influence your expression of your birthchart and as a result affect your t-square. Some influences, because of the planet or aspect involved, are easier than others, but all may help you to develop the awareness or the motivation necessary to use your t-square energies constructively.

A planet (whether by transit, progression or via the chart of another person) which conjuncts your focal planet will blend with it and alter its expression according to: 1) the nature of the influencing planet; 2) the sign, house, aspects and house ruled by it in your natal chart or the chart of the person in question; 3) how these two planets function together; 4) how you respond to its energies. This is one of your best opportunities for experimenting with new ways of expressing your focal planet. If you don't take charge of this influence, it is likely to take charge of you. If the planets are related in meaning (such as Pluto/ Mars, Moon/Neptune or Jupiter/Uranus), you may become even more unbalanced and extreme, because the influencing planet fuels and exaggerates your focal planet. You may, on the other hand, be even more motivated to express the highest dimensions of your focal planet. If the planets are quite different in nature (such as Saturn/Uranus, Sun/Moon or Venus/Mars) you may learn to modify the expression of your focal planet or to channel its energies more effectively.

A conjunction to one of the opposing planets of your t-square will have a similar influence. But because it will shift the focus of your t-square from the focal planet to the planet being aspected, the square between these two planets may become increasingly problematic; you may also have difficulty integrating the other end of the opposition. You need to actively express the planet that is being aspected, but unless you incorporate into its expression an awareness of the needs of the other planets in your t-square, you are likely to experience the boomerang effect of shifting into the other side of the opposition when the transit or progression ends, or the person in question disappears from your life.

A planet in trine or sextile to your focal planet will provide an easy outlet for the expression of the focal planet, provided that you: 1) take advantage of the aspect being formed; 2) express these two planets in relation to each other; 3) direct the energies of your focal planet toward the sign and house of the aspecting planet, and vice versa. This trine or sextile can lead you to believe that the dilemmas of your t-square are resolved; they may be - *temporarily*. However, unless you pay attention to this influence and learn from it how you can effectively express your focal planet, you may re-experience the original conflict when this transit or progression ends or when this person whose planet trines or sextiles your planet also departs from your life. A planet trine or sextile another planet in your t-square will operate in a similar manner, but its effect will not be as significant.

A frequently overlooked influence upon the t-square is that of a planet at the near or far midpoint of one of its squares. Although such a planet increases the tension in your t-square by creating semi-squares and sesquiquadrates, it often acts as a funnel, allowing you to moderate and channel the energies of your t-square by taking advantage of new opportunities that are available to you.

Probably the most important influence upon your t-square is that of a planet opposing your focal planet and filling in the empty space. Such a planet creates

a grand cross. It may enable you to center yourself,
to achieve balance in your life and to integrate all
your planetary energies. Or, it may paralyze you, because you are now torn in four directions rather than
three, and are no longer driven to overemphasize your
focal planet; however, only by stopping and reassessing
your life and your behavior can you hope to end wasteful and outdated patterns of being and to develop new
and more satisfying patterns. Your response to this
influence depends upon your awareness and your urge to
further your own development, as well as upon the nature of the aspect and all the planets involved in
your t-square. An outer planet transit, an eclipse or
a progression crossing your empty space is usually more
difficult to deal with than the influence of a planet
in another person's chart. The differences between
these influences will be considered later in this chapter. Planets positioned in your empty sign and house
which do not oppose your focal planet can also help
you to overcome the deficiencies of your empty space.

When interpreting planetary influences, pay particular attention to the aspects made by your focal
planet as it transits your chart and moves forward or
backward by progression; note also the aspects made to
your chart by the same planet in the charts of people
close to you. These aspects will attune you to a wide
range of possibilities open to you in expressing this
planet. Aspects made by the ruler of your empty sign
or house can also help you to develop and apply the energies of that sign or house. Even when the ruler does
not aspect your t-square, it may have an indirect but
favorable effect upon it if strongly positioned - conjunct an angle or important planet in your chart or in
its own sign or house. Whether operating as a transit,
a progression, or another person's planet in relation
to that person's chart or in relation to your own
chart, it can help you to become aware of and to develop the qualities of your empty space.

One other influence which merits your attention
is that of aspects made between the planets which occur in your t-square. If, for example, you have a t-
square involving Moon, Neptune and Mars, you can be-

gin to integrate these energies by observing, utilizing and learning from aspects made by transiting or progressed Mars or another person's Mars to your Moon and Neptune, by Neptune to your Moon and Mars, and by the Moon to your Mars and Neptune.

Any planet and any aspect can influence you positively or negatively. Saturn can lead to increased productivity and/or to depression and isolation. Neptune can introduce you to spiritual or creative heights and/or cloud your vision so that you are unable to make wise decisions. But before considering the influence of each planet, you should understand, more specifically, how transits, lunations, eclipses, progressions, solar return charts and the planets of other people in your life affect your t-square.

Transits, Eclipses and Lunations

You are likely to experience a transit as an external influence until you have come to terms with its energies and incorporated it consciously into your life. A conjunction made by an outer planet transit is the most profound in its effect. Frequently, you will experience it on the periphery of your consciousness, and feel disturbed by its energies until the transit is exact. Once you identify with the transiting planet, learn its lessons, and begin to express it in accordance with the planet being aspected, you will experience the transit as liberating rather than merely upsetting.

If, for example, transiting Saturn is approaching your focal Venus, you may at first feel isolated and emotionally and materially deprived. However, once you have confronted these feelings, you may be able to apply yourself productively to an artistic project without minding the hours alone; you may find that work done conscientiously in the past is finally beginning to bring material rewards; or you may begin slowly and cautiously to establish a love relationship which has the potential to endure.

When a transit aspects both planets involved in a square or opposition in your t-square, you may be

136

WHAT HAPPENED WHEN...?
Focal Planet Conjunctions

Transiting Pluto conjuncted a woman's *focal Neptune* in
  Libra in the 1st house? She got married. Neptune
  rules her 7th house.

Transiting Pluto conjuncted a girl's *focal Neptune* in
  Cancer in the 2nd house? She was forced to leave her
  home country alone at age 15, wrestled with poverty
  and starvation, developed self-reliance and experienced an unhappy 1½ month marriage. Transiting Pluto
  was exactly squaring her Sun in Aries in the 11th
  house, which rules her 4th house.

Transiting Uranus conjuncted a young man's *focal Saturn*
  in Scorpio in the 2nd house? Under his father's influence, he gave up his carefree surfing life and
  entered the navy. He was miserable there. Saturn
  rules his 5th house; Uranus rules his 6th. The same
  week, transiting Saturn crossed his ascendant.

Transiting Jupiter conjuncted a woman's *focal Venus* in
  Gemini in the 7th house? She broke free of an unsatisfying sexual relationship with an older married
  man - her therapist.

Transiting Saturn conjuncted a woman's *focal Pluto* in
  Leo in the 11th house? She became actively involved
  in dance classes, which became an important outlet
  for coping with anxiety and tension. This woman has
  a combination t-square/grand cross with Venus in
  Pisces in the 5th and a Mars/Saturn opposition.

Transiting Mars made its biyearly return over a woman's
  focal Mars in Virgo rising? She was in a motorcycle
  accident. Mars rules her 8th house.

Transiting Saturn conjuncted a man's *focal Moon* in Virgo
  in the 8th house? He was sued for not paying child
  support, he declared bankruptcy and he established
  a serious relationship with a wealthy woman. Saturn
  is in his natal 7th house and rules his 1st house;
  the Moon rules his descendant.

Transiting Jupiter conjuncted a man's *focal Pluto* in
  Cancer in the 8th house? He received a large grant
  for educational research and separated from his wife.
  Pluto rules his 1st house; natal Jupiter is in his
  10th house and rules his 2nd house.

Focal Planet Conjunctions continued

The Progressed Moon conjuncted a woman's *focal Uranus*
in Cancer in the 4th house? She left home at age 18
to live with a man.

Transiting Saturn conjuncted her *focal Uranus*? She
moved and established her second long-term relationship. Saturn is descending in her natal chart.

Transiting Saturn made its return over a man's *focal
Saturn* in Cancer in the 6th house? He was fired from
an insurance job which he hated, was unemployed, and
then went back into the same field in order to maintain a love relationship.

Transiting Jupiter conjuncted his *focal Saturn* in the
6th house? He began chiropractic treatment for back
trouble. Saturn rules his ascendant.

Transiting Pluto conjuncted a woman's *focal Mercury* in
Libra in the 8th house? Her child died. Mercury rules
her 5th house. Transiting Pluto was squaring her opposition between Moon in Capricorn in the 11th and
Pluto in Cancer in the 5th.

The Progressed Moon conjuncted a woman's *focal Sun* in
Pisces in the 6th? She became active in a feminist
spiritual group. The Sun rules her 11th house.

Transiting Jupiter conjuncted a woman's *focal Saturn*
in Cancer in the 4th house? Several months later,
her Progressed Moon conjuncted Saturn. Her first
child was born between these two influences.

Focal Planet Oppositions

Transiting Pluto in the 2nd house opposed a woman's
focal Mercury in Aries in the 8th? She battled with
her ex-husband over alimony payments and began a
satisfying career as a birth control counselor.

Transiting Pluto in the 12th house opposed the midpoint
of a woman's *focal Sun/Mercury* conjunction in Aries
in the 6th while Jupiter conjuncted her Moon in Cancer in the 9th (also involved in her t-square)? She
entered group therapy to discover why she worked
compulsively and isolated herself.

The Progressed Moon in the 12th house opposed a man!s *focal Saturn* in Cancer in the 6th? He quit a real estate job and was unemployed for several months.

Transiting Uranus in the 5th house opposed a woman's *focal Jupiter* in Scorpio in the 11th? Her family moved, and she was unhappy. Natal Uranus occurs in (and rules) her 3rd house; Jupiter rules her 1st.

Transiting Saturn in the 5th house opposed her *focal Jupiter*? Her family moved again, from Europe to the U.S., and she enthusiastically applied herself to learning the customs of her new country.

Transiting Saturn in the 6th house opposed a man's *focal Neptune* in Libra in the 12th house, squaring Saturn in Cancer in the 9th and Mercury in Capricorn in the 3rd? He attempted suicide.

Transiting Saturn in the 6th house opposed a woman's *focal Mercury* in Gemini in the 12th? She quit high school during a successful senior year because she was pregnant, got married and had a baby. Her husband's Sun and Venus conjunct the empty space of her t-square. Natal Saturn in her 11th house rules her 7th; Mercury rules her 4th.

The Progressed Moon in the 1st house opposed a Jewish woman's *focal Uranus* in Cancer in the 7th? She entered her first serious relationship with an Arab.

The Progressed Ascendant in the 1st house opposed her *focal Uranus* in Cancer in the 7th? She started a long-term relationship with a double Capricorn man.

Transiting Mars in the 6th house opposed a woman's *focal Mercury* in the 12th? She was involved in a car accident while moving to another state. Mars in Cancer is rising in her chart; Mercury rules her 4th.

Transiting Neptune in the 2nd house opposed a woman's *focal Moon* in Gemini in the 8th house? She was robbed by two women.

Transiting Saturn in the 12th house opposed a woman's *focal Sun* in Pisces in the 6th house? She experienced an "opening up" of work opportunities and found satisfaction as a massage therapist and counselor.

most aware of its effect upon you when it reaches the
midpoint of the two planets. For example, if your Sun
at 18 Leo opposes your Moon at 24 Aquarius, you may be
at the peak of the influence of transiting Uranus when
Uranus reaches 21 Scorpio, even if your focal planet
is not positioned at this degree. When a transiting
planet is stationary in aspect to a t-square planet,
its influence may be the most dramatic; it will then
require you to confront and assimilate its energies.

Outer planets aspecting your t-square are more
significant than inner planets, although several inner
planets simultaneously forming an aspect may affect
you powerfully, particularly if they accompany a related transit by an outer planet. Of all the inner
planet transits, those which correspond to your focal
planet or the ruler of your empty sign or house may be
the most important; Mars, in particular, can trigger
a new beginning in your life if you are motivated to
take wise action.

Outer planet transits conjunct or opposing your
focal planet frequently make an exact aspect several
times, bringing about crises which, once dealt with,
usually reveal beneficial consequences. Do not make
the mistake of passively awaiting the rewards of Jupiter, for Jupiter exaggerates the circumstances occurring in the area of your life it is influencing, and
if you are not taking care of yourself or fulfilling
your responsibilities here, Jupiter may not be the
blessing you expected. Although Jupiter is rarely as
powerful as the other outer planets, it too must be
applied and directed.

When interpreting a transit, pay attention to the
nature of the transiting planet, its position natally
and by transit, and the aspect it is forming. This
transit will influence not only the natal planet it is
aspecting, according to its position by sign and house,
but also the house it rules in your chart, particularly
if that house is not tenanted by planets.

Note also whenever a transit (especially an outer
planet) forms another t-square in your chart by squar-

ing and opposing planets involved in a square that is not part of your t-square, or by squaring both planets of a natal opposition. Whether the transiting or natal planet becomes the focal planet of this temporary t-square, pay attention to how you express it; do not neglect to cultivate the sign and house of the temporary empty space.

Two other kinds of transits influence your t-square - lunations and eclipses. When the degree of the New Moon exactly aspects a planet in your t-square, it can indicate the start of a new cycle in regard to the expression of this planet. Even more important are aspects made by solar and lunar eclipses. An eclipse occurring within one degree of a planet or significant midpoint in your t-square will usually trigger your entire t-square, often precipitating a crisis related to the meaning of your focal planet. Eclipses conjunct your t-square are rarely easy influences, but in the long run, may lead to highly favorable developments. Eclipses trine your t-square planets often introduce new opportunities which may help you to actualize the potential of your t-square.

Secondary Progressions

Secondary progressions,* based upon each day after birth indicating one year of life, operate like outer planet transits; their influence, however, is usually more internal and subjective, affecting attitudes and approaches even more than external circumstances.

Your t-square will be especially powerful if its planets (particularly the focal planet) are moving into exact aspect by progression, rather than separating from an exact aspect; it will increase in strength until each of its squares becomes exact by progression. If, for example, your t-square involves an opposition between 14 Gemini and 14 Sagittarius and focal Jupiter is 8 Virgo, your progressed Jupiter will form an exact

---

* *Primary and solar progressions also similarly influence the t-square configuration.*

A CASE STUDY:
Transits and Progressions

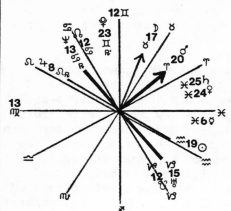

This chart contains a t-square to Mars in Aries in the 8th house, with a Uranus/Neptune opposition conjunct the nodal axis. Focal Mars is in its own sign. The empty space is Libra in the 2nd house, ruled by Venus in Pisces in the 7th house.

A second weak t-square involves a Sun/Jupiter opposition (somewhat out of orb) in square to Moon in Taurus in the 9th house. This is a t-square only because the Sun and Moon are involved. The focal Moon rules the 11th house. The empty space is Scorpio in the 3rd house, ruled by Pluto in Gemini in the 10th house.

These t-squares are linked. Focal Mars at the Pluto/Sun midpoint, sextiles both Pluto and the Sun. Focal Moon, trining Uranus and weakly sextiling Neptune, provides an outlet for the Uranus/Neptune opposition.

The following tables list the significant events that occurred in this man's life, under the influence of transits, secondary progressions and eclipses forming conjunctions, oppositions and trines to his focal planets. Although these tables describe external circumstances in his life and do not fully indicate the psychological ramifications of these circumstances, they do reveal which of a wide range of possibilities he responded to and/or actualized during the course of 71 years. Note that for this man, as for everyone, trines are not always easy influences, and oppositions often result in favorable events or actions.

A CASE STUDY:
T-Square to Mars

Progressed Venus conjunct Mars (1930) Financial
struggle. Completed law degree after Depression
began.

*Transiting Uranus and progressed Moon conjunct Mars
(1932-33)* - Worked for a law firm without receiving pay. Finally started his own law firm. Remained a confirmed bachelor.

*Progressed Ascendant opposition Mars, transiting
North Node conjunct Mars (1949)* - Married for the
first and only time. (His wife's South Node and
Moon conjunct his Mars; her North Node is in his
empty space. Her Venus and Neptune in Leo trine
his Mars.)

*Transiting Pluto in the 12th house trine Mars (1950-
51)* - Profitable investments. Birth of first child.

Transiting Saturn and Neptune opposition Mars (1952)-
Hard work. Active in community affairs. Responsibilities of two children.

Solar eclipse at 19 Libra opposition Mars (1958) -
Unsound investments. Bought motels in Key West a
few years before influx of Cuban refugees. Mort-
gage payments on large new home in Miami. Beginning of financial difficulties.

*Progressed Moon conjunct Mars, transiting Uranus in
Leo in 12th house trine Mars (1960-61)* - Wife seriously ill with rheumatic fever, leading to open
heart surgery.

Progressed Sun conjunct Mars (1969-70) - Financial
increase. Paying off debts. Death of mother.

Transiting Uranus opposition Mars (1972-73) - Less
involved in work. Unfocused. Preparing to retire.

*Transiting Neptune in Sagittarius in the 4th house
and progressed Midheaven in Leo in the 12th house
trine Mars (1978-79)* - Attempting to emerge from
an unhappy retirement. Real estate investments.
Living half the year in a second home in the mountains.

*UPCOMING TRANSITS (1979-80) - Transiting Neptune
trine Mars again, transiting Pluto in Libra opposition Mars.*

A CASE STUDY:
T-Square to Moon (weak)

Solar eclipse conjunct Moon (1929) – Major disappointment when unable to manage and travel with university football team. Result: completed law degree.

Transiting Uranus conjunct Moon (1939) – Health problems. Leader in the development of the Key West overseas highway. Escorted F.D.R. across it.

Progressed Mars conjunct Moon (1946-47) – Returned from war. Stayed at naval medical center because of adjustment difficulties. Met future wife. (Her Capricorn ascendant and Mercury in Virgo trine his Moon.)

Progressed Moon opposition Moon (1950) – Birth of first child a year after marriage.

Progressed Venus conjunct Moon (1952-53) – Successfully applied to open a savings and loan association. Trips to Washington D.C. Second child born.

Transiting Neptune opposition Moon, transiting Jupiter conjunct Moon and progressed Moon return (1964) – Most difficult year of life. Wife seriously ill, recuperating from open heart surgery. Loss of resources invested in Key West motels. Major crisis in group relationships at work leading to dissolution of friendships and partial retirement.

Transiting Pluto and Uranus in Virgo in 1st house trine Moon (1965-66) – Unhappy in work. Major trip to Europe and Russia.

Transiting Saturn conjunct Moon, transiting Jupiter opposition Moon (1970) – Death of mother.

Solar eclipse conjunct Moon, progressed Moon return, transiting Uranus and progressed ascendant opposition Moon, progressed Uranus stationary in Capricorn in 5th house in exact trine to Moon (1977-79) – Continuing problems with colitis. Upset over childrens' sudden and difficult relationship break-ups and subsequent court battles. Established second home in North Carolina. Traveled frequently between homes and to California to help eldest son. Purchased and sold land. Decided to sell Miami home.

UPCOMING INFLUENCES: Transiting Saturn followed by Jupiter in Virgo trine Moon, progressed Uranus turning retrograde in exact trine to Moon.

t-square to your natal opposition when it reaches 14
Virgo, probably when you are in your thirties if Jupiter does not turn retrograde. Outer planets involved
in your t-square, unless widely separating, usually
remain strong in influence for many years of your life
because they move so slowly by progression. (When determining when outer planet progressions become exact,
use small orbs, preferably less than 15 minutes.) Inner
planet progressions, because they move more quickly,
may eventually trine or sextile themselves or other t-
square planets; during these periods, you may be able
to discover and take advantage of new channels for the
expression of these energies.

Note also when planets involved in your t-square
(particularly the focal planet) change signs and houses
by progression. Such changes will direct you toward expressing these planets in new ways and applying their
influence to other areas of your life.

When any progressed planet or angle aspects your
t-square, whether or not the planet is involved in the
natal configuration, you will experience new challenges,
opportunities or outlets related to the nature and position of the progressed planet and t-square planet.
Aspects formed by progressed outer planets will remain
in effect for many years; by the Sun, Mercury, Venus
and Mars, for one or two years (usually from a little
less than one degree before the exact aspect to nearly
a degree afterwards); and by the progressed Moon, for
two months. The progressed Moon may only have a significant influence upon your t-square when it conjuncts, opposes or trines your focal planet. Because it may create
an instinctive identification with this planetary energy,
provide an easy channel for its expression, or help you
to regain your balance, you may want to pay attention
to its influence.

Whether or not your progressed focal planet aspects
your t-square, it will be quite powerful when it becomes
strongly positioned in your chart - particularly when it
conjuncts an angle or another planet or enters its own
sign or house. The increased influence of the ruler of
your empty space as it progresses across important areas

of your chart, and the influence of planets moving into the sign or house of your empty space will also help you to overcome deficiencies indicated by your empty sign and house.

Stationary and Retrograde Motion

Even more important than a progressed planet aspecting your t-square is the change in direction of your focal planet to retrograde* or direct motion. Retrograde planets, whether natally or by progression, indicate functions which you must evaluate, re-work or develop in your own unique way before expressing outwardly. Frequently, like 12th house planets, they denote facets of yourself which were not encouraged by your parents and which, as a result, remain latent or operate on a psychological level. Retrograde planets not only indicate energies directed inward; they also delay outward expression, and sometimes function in an indirect, compulsive or otherwise unconscious manner. They do, nevertheless, give you not only the ability to understand the nature of that planetary energy, but also the self-motivation to express it in accordance with your inner voice.

A retrograde focal planet will generally create fewer external problems than a direct focal planet, but will strongly affect your feelings, thoughts, attidues and/or physical body. It is not likely to remain retrograde for many years of your life. Because many of the possible expressions of your t-square remain latent during the years in which your focal planet is retrograde, its change of direction will have a dramatic effect upon you. The psychological crisis which you experience during the stationary period will realign your energies so that you may begin to outwardly express the conflicts and capabilities of that planet which have been developing inside you, and to

---

* *A planet is retrograde when, because of the relationship between its orbit and the earth's orbit, it appears to be moving backwards. The Sun and Moon are never retrograde.*

146

translate the awareness you gained during the retrograde period into overt action.

If your focal planet is direct and turns retrograde, the external circumstances affected by your t-square may resolve themselves, or at least become less problematic. Sometimes, the house which the planet rules in your chart, rather than the house in which it is positioned, becomes the primary source of stress in your life. Once retrograde, your focal planet will operate according to its retrograde meaning more than its direct meaning. You will become attuned to the inner dimensions of this planet, and much of your energy will be turned inward as you begin to evaluate and understand the areas of your life which it influences. Occasionally, if a t-square is strong, the inward manifestations of a focal planet turning retrograde affect the physical body, resulting in health problems which usually cannot be overcome until the conflicts associated with this planet are confronted and resolved.

The length of time during which a planet is stationary turning direct or stationary turning retrograde varies, depending upon the nature of the planet. An outer planet may remain at the same degree and minute for many years. The stationary periods of your focal planet are usually the most important and most difficult periods in your life, because the energy so intensively released through your focal planet is preparing to be totally redirected. You may, when and if your focal planet is stationary, become obsessed with or dominated by its effect upon you; you may express it compulsively and inappropriately; you may lean heavily into your empty space, attempting to escape from the tension you experience; you may feel blocked, at a complete standstill in regard to the expression of this planet, sign and house. This period is indeed a challenging one, and often leads to an awakening which, in time, can enable you to actualize the highest potential of your t-square. Pay attention to the aspects your focal planet forms (particularly to t-square planets) when it is stationary, because these aspects can indicate channels through which you can release the pent-up energy of this stationary period.

STATIONARY & RETROGRADE INFLUENCES

Mercury

STATIONARY PERIOD: 6-12 months by progression
crisis in thinking, communication, interaction
overly mental; circular thinking; detailed
must process, analyze & assimilate experience
compulsive in speech; difficulty making contact
inner nervousness & restlessness

RETROGRADE PERIOD: 20-25 years by progression
contemplative; concerned with mental processes
mentally hyperactive; easily stimulated, overloaded
literary; attuned to imagery; writing ability
intuitive; attuned to universal levels
aware of subtleties, atmosphere, hidden messages
absentminded; overlooks external details
introspective; self-analytical; self-critical
doubts mental & verbal abilities; anxious
natal: thinking/communication discouraged by parents
difficulty making contact with people or environment
alternately overly communicative & uncommunicative
indirect or disconnected communication

Venus

STATIONARY PERIOD: 6-12 months by progression
crisis in values, love, personal relationships
focusing upon relationships and love
evaluating; assessing social & material needs
striving to be liked; cultivating pleasant demeanor
highly artistic; conscious of inner & outer beauty

RETROGRADE PERIOD: 40-43 years by progression
solitary; withdrawing from relationships; ascetic
turning inward for emotional satisfaction
desiring to please self; unconcerned with appearances
narcissistic; self-indulgent; abnormal appetites
aesthetic sensitivity; attuned to inner beauty
evaluating; developing own unique value system
reflective about relationships & love
socially unconventional; dislikes social rituals
dissatisfied with ordinary love relationships
values uncommon or unique qualities in others
feels unworthy of love; oversensitive to others
difficulty giving or receiving love
natal: felt unloved as child; undemonstrative parents
unmaterialistic; unusual material tastes

Mars

STATIONARY PERIOD: *1-2 years by progression*
crisis in regard to action & release of energy
hyperactive; energetic; driving
pushy; forceful; overly aggressive
highly sexual or physical
preoccupied with own desires & activities
preparing for a new beginning
RETROGRADE PERIOD: *60-80 years by progression*
slow to act; must carefully assess actions
unassertive; difficulty satisfying desires
feels beaten; doubts capacity to succeed; fears to act
natal: feels abused; fears to initiate
subconscious motivations & desires
acts indirectly; behind the scenes accomplishments
inspired action; actions motivated by ideals or cause
emotional energy; actively explores the psyche
pent-up anger; easily frustrated; defensive
alternately passive/unmotivated & explosive/driving
sexually dominating or unarousable; sexually repressed
self-destructive; self-abusing; accident-prone
competes with self; threatened by external competition

Jupiter

STATIONARY PERIOD: *2-3 years by progression*
crisis in understanding, direction, social orientation
must develop & impart understanding; philosophical
preoccupied with the future; overly optimistic
overextended; difficulty assimilating experience
changing direction; preparing to turn inward/outward
RETROGRADE PERIOD: *118-124 years by progression*
faith in self; attuned to inner abundance
developing inner wisdom; reflective; exploring psyche
seeking understanding; philosophical
spiritual rather than religious; upholds principles
developing personal belief system & ethics
protects insights/understanding; hoards inner wealth
natal: rejects parents' social & belief structure
perspective; focusing upon own future; planning
enjoying own company; neither outgoing nor generous
oriented toward taking in rather than giving out
mentally overloaded; needs "space" to assimilate
unconsciously demanding; unconsciously materialistic

Saturn
STATIONARY PERIOD: 4-5 years by progression
crisis affecting work, responsibility, self-control
confronting obstacles/limitations; coming to adulthood
coping with pain, loss, isolation; developing strength
overly controlling, disciplined or self-denying
preoccupied with security, responsibility, success
driven to achieve; overly ambitious; compulsive worker
RETROGRADE PERIOD: 134-142 years by progression
self-denying; stoical; excessively demanding of self
feels inadequate or inferior; self-doubting; fearful
negative; melancholy; expects failure; overly cautious
natal: weak father; family lacked order, discipline
feels isolated; needs to retreat
self-controlled; inhibited; closed; blocks self
weak defenses but inner rigidity; resists change
coping with pain, fear, loss, limitation; stamina
conquering inner obstacles; "working" on problems
desiring psychological rather than external security
threatened by competition; difficulties with authority
self-motivated in work; prefers to work alone
alternately avoids work and works compulsively

Uranus
STATIONARY PERIOD: 5-8 years by progression
crisis affecting individuality, freedom, mental health
alienated; detached; questioning role in society
preoccupied with metaphysics or social reform
breaking free of restrictions; rebellious; transforming
flashes of insight; mental bombardment; eccentricity
extreme ups & downs; instability; questioning sanity
RETROGRADE PERIOD: 148-154 years by progression
intuitive; attuned to universal levels
thinks for oneself; original ideas
follows inner guidance; attuned to inner voice
resists outside influences; needs psychological freedom
psychological/metaphysical orientation
feels alienated from others; at odds with society
self-transforming; changing self rather than society
outwardly conventional but inwardly individualistic
natal: parents discouraged individuality/freedom
nervous; continually stimulated by psyche
rebels without cause; rebels against self
idiosyncratic behavior; extremes of temperament

Neptune
STATIONARY PERIOD: *6-8 years by progression*
crisis affecting ideals, spirituality, creativity
concerned with spiritual or creative service
overcome with confusion; lack of clarity
overly active imagination; creative; inspired
seeking otherworldly experiences; lost in fantasy
physically and emotionally oversensitive
period of transition and emotional flux
RETROGRADE PERIOD: *154-161 years by progression*
attuned to inner vision; open to inspiration
highly absorbent; impressionable
active fantasy and dream life
unconsciously directed by fantasies & dreams
difficulty separating reality & fantasy
difficulty translating ideals into practical action
emotionally confused; self-deluding
escapes into inner world; inclined to "get high"
physically and psychically oversensitive
spiritual; capable of transcending self
natal: family discouraged creativity/spirituality

Pluto
STATIONARY PERIOD: *6-8 years by progression*
crisis affecting expression of power & sexuality
high intensity; powerful emotions
passionate; overcome by desires; sexually obsessed
compulsive; fixated; feels out of control
explosive; aggressive; forceful; confrontative
making drastic changes; overthrowing old patterns
alienated; unable to connect with others
driven to penetrate beneath the surface of reality
RETROGRADE PERIOD: *156-162 years by progression*
explorer of the psyche; penetrating awareness
able to confront and transform self
inner power and intensity; emotional extremes
inner upheavals and transformations
powerful repressed desires; pent-up energy
natal: family was a repressive influence
concerned with controlling emotions & passions
represses emotions then explodes uncontrollably
compulsive; self-destructive; self-judging
private; feels psychologically isolated

If a planet other than your focal planet turns direct or retrograde, you will experience similar influences, but the focal area of your t-square will not be quite as profoundly affected. If a planet outside your t-square reverses direction, it will influence the areas of your life affected by your t-square, if natally or by progression it aspects t-square planets.

The preceding tables indicate some of the energies that you might experience when a planet in your t-square turns stationary and then retrograde by progression. They also describe possible manifestations of any planet which is stationary or retrograde in your natal chart.

Solar Returns

Your solar return is a yearly chart calculated for the minute the Sun returns to its natal position. Describing your energies and your orientation during any given year, the solar return is a powerful tool for understanding the unfoldment of your natal chart; it clarifies the meaning of transits and progressions and reveals significant influences which these transits and progressions may fail to indicate.

One of the most helpful uses of the solar return is as a guide to channelling the energies of natal aspects. Look to the planets in square and opposition in your natal chart, especially those involved in your t-square. What is their relationship in your solar return? The years in which your solar return contains close conjunctions (or trines or sextiles) between two planets in square or opposition natally are years in which you can experience these planets operating constructively together. With the conjunction in particular, you may learn lessons which help you to resolve the dilemmas denoted by your t-square.

Where, in your solar return chart, is the focal planet of your natal t-square? Here, by sign and house, you must apply its energies. If on an angle, in its own sign or house, or in its natal sign, house or degree, its influence will be powerful throughout the year.

What happens to the sign and house of your natal empty space, and to the rulers of its sign and house? If either ruler is strongly positioned in your solar return, this will be a year for developing its characteristics. If your solar return contains planets in the sign or house of your natal empty space, these planets can help you to overcome the deficiencies denoted here.

Are the focal planet and empty space ruler* of your natal chart in aspect in your solar return? If in opposition or square, you will experience conflict between them, but will be motivated to integrate them. If in conjunction, sextile or trine, such integration may occur easily, but you will need to be aware of how it occurs if you are to continue to express these planets together harmoniously when your solar return year ends.

If you have a t-square in your solar return, it will not be as significant or as potent as your natal t-square, but it will operate in a similar fashion. Note where the focal planet of this t-square occurs natally; its natal influence will be channelled through the solar return sign and house. You will overemphasize that planet, sign and house during the year, and will need to develop the solar return empty space, integrating it with the focal planet position.

Lunar returns, monthly charts calculated for the minute the Moon returns to its natal position, are interpreted like solar returns; they also indicate periods of time (months) in which you may most successfully integrate t-square planets. Lunar returns are particularly useful tools for people who have the Moon emphasized natally – as a focal planet, on an angle, or in its own sign or house.

----

*Although the rulers of the empty sign and empty house are both significant in relation to the t-square, the ruler of the empty sign usually most reflects the deficiencies of the empty space.

Chart Comparisons

Your expression of your t-square is also influenced
by the dynamics of your personal relationships. The natal planets of the significant people in your life may
conjunct, oppose, trine or sextile planets in your t-
square, creating new channels of energy or activating
and redirecting existing channels, as indicated by your
natal aspects. The planets in another person's chart
which aspect your t-square will function like the same
planets making the same aspect to your t-square by
transit, but you will experience these energies in relation to the person in question.

The beginning of this chapter describes the influences of various aspects upon your t-square, but does
not specifically discuss the meaning of these aspects
as they occur between charts. With people who have
planets conjunct your t-square planets (particularly
your focal planet), you are likely to experience close
connections. Because they will stimulate you by rein-
forcing your natal planets and aspects, they are likely to activate your t-square energies and require you
to face the conflicts indicated by your particular
configuration. Although you may experience a common
bond with these people, you must be wary of allowing
them to pull you even more off center. Much depends
upon the nature of the planetary contact. A person's
Saturn conjuncting your focal Uranus may be a stabilizing (as well as restrictive) influence, but Mars
conjuncting your focal Uranus may incline you to become even more erratic, self-willed and rebellious.

With people who have planets in trine or sextile to
your t-square planets (particularly your focal planet),
you will experience an ease of self-expression. With
them, many of the problems in your life will seem to
evaporate. Everything will be easier, more flowing,
less frustrating. These people are likely to have a
soothing effect upon you and to direct you to express
your energies constructively, in a manner related to
their aspecting planet and where it falls in your natal chart. You must, however, be careful not to lean
too heavily upon them. Their support can weaken you,

and keep you from resolving the conflicts in your life, or it can strengthen you and enable you to more freely and easily continue with your own development.

People who have planets in the empty space of your t-square (or to a lesser extent, who have planets in a different sign, but in the empty house) are likely to have a significant influence upon you. You may even gravitate toward them, because they personify qualities which you lack. These people will help you to regain your balance and to overcome the deficiencies of your empty space, although your interactions with them will not always be easy. Because they activate your t-square, they force you to grow and develop new patterns of behavior. You must, however, be wary of relying upon them to balance you or to express the empty area of your t-square for you. Unless you incorporate these qualities into yourself, you will discover that the problems represented by your t-square are reawakened when these people no longer influence your life.

People are complex, and influenced by a variety of planets, signs and houses. With those people who have one or more planets conjuncting your t-square, trining or sextiling it *and also* opposing your focal planet, you will probably experience the greatest compatibility. You will benefit in particular from interactions with people who have an emphasis of one or more of three signs - the two signs trining your focal planet, and the sign of your empty space.

Apart from chart comparisons, the composite chart, based upon the midpoints between planets in two or more natal charts, can influence how you express your t-square. Conjunctions, trines or sextiles occurring in the composite chart of one of your relationships, and linking two planets which are in square or opposition in your natal chart, can indicate that this relationship clearly has the potential for bringing these two facets of yourself into harmony. A t-square in a composite chart functions in a similar manner to a natal t-square, and can destroy the rapport between two people if the empty area of the composite chart is not cultivated and the energies involved in the t-square synthesized and channelled constructively.

Nodes and Angles

Whatever aspect a planet makes to your t-square, whether by transit or progression or through the influence of another person, it urges you to integrate the lessons of that planet with the lessons of the planet it is aspecting. Because the favorable and unfavorable dimensions of each planet are described in the chapter on focal planets, they need not be covered here. However, aspects formed by the ascendant, midheaven and lunar nodes also indicate potential channels of expression for t-square planets, and should be considered.

Your progressed ascendant or another person's ascendant aspecting a t-square planet inclines you to identify with that planet and to express it outwardly. The influence of this planet, as it occurs by sign or house in your chart, may dominate your consciousness and alter your awareness. It influences your perception of yourself and your direction in life; it also affects your energy flow and your contact with your physical body. This planet may, when not integrated with your other planets, lead to problems with health or self-expression, or it may allow you to experience an outpouring of energy - energy related to this planet's particular nature and its position in your chart.

Your progressed midheaven or another person's midheaven aspecting one of your t-square planets influences your orientation toward the public and your professional goals and activities. By inclining you to incorporate the energies of this planet into your public life, it may provide opportunities for considerable achievement.

Aspects formed to your t-square by the transiting lunar nodes (and also by the progressed nodes, which can in the course of a lifetime weaken or strengthen an aspect) also influence your t-square. South Node conjunctions may bring into your life people or experiences from the past which enable you to draw from the energies of the aspecting planet, but do not necessarily further your own development. North Node conjunctions direct you, through an interpersonal connection or through new experiences, to express the highest potential of the planet being aspected. When the North Node crosses your empty space, you can derive the most benefit from focusing upon this area of your life; when the South Node crosses your empty space, you may be inclined to retreat into your empty sign and house, but you need to pay attention to the constructive expression of your focal planet. Trines and sextiles formed by the nodal axis to your t-square planets are not very significant, but can help you to use the resources of the South Node's sign and house to channel the energy of the aspected planet into the sign and house of the North Node.

Aspects formed by the lunar axis of other people to your t-square planets influence them more than you, suggesting ways in which you incline them to draw from their past resources, as indicated by their South Node, and to struggle with or begin to fulfill the important life task indicated by their North Node.

HOW TO HANDLE YOUR T-SQUARE: THEORY

If you are reading this book because you have a t-square, you are most likely attempting to understand yourself and to discover how you can express the energies represented by your t-square more effectively. Studying the planets, signs and houses involved in your t-square can help you to become aware of how they are operating in your life and to intellectually explore alternative ways of being. Understanding *can* change your life, to the extent that it widens your perspective, reveals new possibilities and enables you to make more conscious choices. But understanding alone is usually not enough to bring about important and enduring changes. You must *want* to change. Your determination to fulfill your potential and to increase your satisfaction in life must be so powerful that you are willing to experience the confusion and even the anguish that may occur when you eliminate negative patterns of behavior and substitute (usually hesitantly and awkwardly at first) new thoughts, actions and experiences.

Every gain is also a loss. Every attempt to direct your future is also a destruction of your past. Even if what you leave behind is unfulfilling, the loss of that behavior, experience or activity is often painful because it has become part of yourself. In order to grow, in order to take the risks of becoming more than you are at present, you must also be willing to leave behind what you have been.

Do you want to change? How severe are the problems associated with your t-square? How distressful? How uncontrollable? How frequently do these problems manifest? Consider, for a moment, the negative manner

158

in which you may be expressing your t-square energies. What is *wrong* with your life?

1) *Are you suffering?*
2) *Are you depressed? Do you lack vitality and motivation? Is your energy blocked?*
3) *Are you unhappy with your relationships and/or activities?*
4) *Do you dislike yourself?*
5) *Does your life lack meaning or purpose?*
6) *Do you feel helpless, mired in patterns of behavior, relationships or activities which are no longer fulfilling?*
7) *Do you feel driven by addictions, compulsions or fixations of any kind?*
8) *Do you frequently feel out of balance or off center?*
9) *Does one area of your life interfere with another, preventing you from functioning well in either area?*
10) *Is your life narrow because you constantly avoid experiences which could arouse fear or anxiety? Do you maintain a rigid lifestyle because you are threatened by unknown possibilities?*
11) *Are you often engaged in warfare with yourself or other people?*
12) *Do you experience health problems which may be psychologically caused?*
13) *Have you unduly emphasized one facet of yourself or one area of your life at the expense of other characteristics or interests?*
14) *Do you experience a wide discrepancy between your accomplishments and your potential? Are you failing to live according to your values? Are you failing to pursue your goals?*

If you answered yes to one or more of the above questions, then you may want to consider how extreme your particular conflict is and how willing you are to invest the energy necessary to resolve it or to make it work for you rather than against you. What do you gain from continuing this pattern? Attention, sympathy, comfort, security, minimal risk? Are you willing to give up this "secondary gain" or discover more constructive ways to achieve the same ends? Are you willing to give up the excitement of a life of extreme fluctuations or frantic activity in order to at least occasionally experience harmony and peace of mind? What are your resistances to changing? What would you lose, and is it important to prevent that loss?

Usually, people do not develop new patterns of behavior when they are preoccupied with the loss of old patterns rather than with the fulfillment which new patterns can bring. Change rarely occurs when you focus upon loss because feelings of anxiety and deprivation prevent you from taking a step forward. To make lasting and significant changes, you must continually focus upon the new behavior, imagining yourself incorporating it into your life and experiencing its rewards. Such focus can motivate you to move toward your personal goals. But first, you must clarify your aim. You must not only want to change and believe that you can change, you must also be able to clearly envision yourself being the person that you want to be.

Mastering Your T-Square

Only you can define the specific nature of the changes you envision. Such definition results from understanding the many variables represented by your t-square, as well as how they operate in relation to each other and how they could operate if each planet, sign, house and aspect were integrated. But this chapter can, nevertheless, help you to conceive of the process and result of synthesizing and channelling these energies, which may now be wasted in internal battles and/or compulsive activity.

As you begin to resolve your inner conflicts, you learn to listen to the voice of each planet, sign and house, and to experience all parts of yourself without judgment. Each part recognizes each other part as valid and no longer desires to dominate your personality. As these various facets of yourself make contact and accept each other, you are able to maintain awareness of the multitude of needs, feelings, thoughts and drives inside of you. You may, for awhile, feel paralyzed by the tensions of conflicting urges. But as your consciousness expands and encompasses all parts of your-

160

> "The old question: who am I (should be) altered
> with the deeper insight into who are I? Only he
> who has selves has self, and only in being true
> to one's selves can one be true to one's self."
>   ANAIS NIN
>
> "Real will is a power, not merely composed of
> various often contradictory desires belonging
> to different 'I's' but issuing from conscious-
> ness and governed by...a single permanent I."
>   GURDJIEFF
>
> "Will is essentially the activity of the self
> which stands above the multiplicity. What is
> loosely called the 'split will' can be recog-
> nized to be the conflict between the central
> will and a multitude of drives, urges, desires
> and wishes....The will is like the conductor
> of an orchestra."   ROBERTO ASSAGIOLI

self, a higher self bursts through the multiplicity,
establishing a center in your chart, and in your consciousness.

Carl Jung refers to this higher self as "the transcendent function." Roberto Assagioli, founder of psychosynthesis, calls it "the will." Gurdjieff, the Rus-
sian mystic, teaches "the law of the three," which,
like the Hegelian dialectic, posits a "reconciling
force" which synthesizes the polarities created by opposing forces.

In your t-square, the opposing forces are your opposing planets, which can be synthesized by the higher
self emerging through your focal planet and expressing
itself in cooperation with your empty sign and house.
In your chart as a whole, the most likely source of
this higher self is the Sun, the center of the solar
system. But although this higher self may emerge
through your Sun or through your focal planet, it issues not merely from these two influences, but rather
from all of your planets operating together. It me-

161

diates the conflicts occurring among your planets,
signs and houses, synthesizing and channelling their
energies and regulating their expression. Functioning
like a conductor of an orchestra, it enables you to
conduct your own planetary symphony and to live in
attunement to its celestial music.

As your higher self develops, each part of yourself is allowed expression and is able to cooperate
with any other part. At any given moment, you are
able to draw from the energies of any or all of your
planets, signs and houses, and to harness that combined energy and awareness to resolve or transcend
whatever conflicts occur in your life, whether related to your t-square or to other planets in or influencing your chart.

The Process of Change

This process of unifying your psyche and developing a higher self is usually not easy. How it occurs
will depend to a large extent upon the positions of
the outer planets in your chart and their influence
by transit and progression, as well as how able you
are to harness their energies. It may require you to
experience the pain of feeling split in two, as you
begin to confront and assimilate conflicting parts
of yourself which you previously shut out of your
awareness. It may demand that you withdraw from some
of your normal activities and turn inward, collect-
ing rather than discharging your energies, allowing
a new self to fuse through psychological heat.

You may be shattered unexpectedly by Uranus,
and forced to rebuild shaky foundations so that you
contact universal levels of yourself and experience
the liberation of breaking free from a binding past.
You may change in a Neptunian manner as you enter
the foggy corridors of your psyche, where distorted
mirrors and blind passages confuse and paralyze you
until you are compelled to discover and follow your
own inner guide.

Before you develop a center, you may have to
learn the lessons of Pluto, planet of transformation.

162

> *"It is bitter indeed to discover behind one's lofty ideals narrow, fanatical convictions...and behind one's heroic pretensions nothing but crude egotism, infantile greed, and complacency...This is an unavoidable stage in every psychotherapeutic process. As the alchemists said, it begins with the nigredo (blackness) or generates it as the indispensable prerequisite for synthesis, for unless the opposites are constellated and brought to consciousness, they can never be united."*
> CARL JUNG

You may have to experience your own lack of a center, to journey into the "black hole" within you and feel the often overwhelming anxiety of confronting your own nothingness. Pluto teaches that the deepest, the most significant, the most enduring changes occur when you enter the vacuum at the core of your being and tap the vast reservoir of energy available there. When fully experienced, the void becomes a "fertile void," as newly discovered energy pours through you. The emptiness gives rise to fullness, the darkness to light. You are reawakened, reborn.

According to the alchemists, who were concerned with the transmutation of both matter and spirit, the process of psychological integration begins with the separation of elements. The atoms of one's being must be split apart in order to be reunited. Because all levels of one's physical being and consciousness must be involved if the integration of the whole self is to occur, the alchemists taught that the major obstacles to psychic transmutation are haste and despair or discouragement. Union must take place on all levels of consciousness; transcendent awareness must penetrate into all areas of life. Therefore, the integration of the psyche takes time, and requires patience and faith. As he discusses alchemy in his superb book, *Maps of Consciousness,* Ralph Metzner explains that psychological union must be born in air (awareness), strengthened in earth (physical experience), treated with water (feeling, compassion) and tested in fire (energy, passion, rage, desire).

163

> "If something is opposed to you and tears you, let it grow; it is that you are taking root and that you are stirring. Blessed is this tearing which causes you to be delivered of yourself, because no truth shows itself and is reached conspicuously... Know that each contradiction without solution, each irreparable dispute obliges you to grow in order to absorb it....For the more a man rises above himself, the greater the height from which he views his disputes and dissensions, until at last they dwindle into nothingness."
> ANTOINE DE ST. EXUPERY

There are many pathways leading to the integration of the psyche. You may be able to develop your higher self without venturing into the darkness; you may, by focusing upon the resolution of the problems represented by your t-square, free yourself of their most negative manifestations, and in the process contact a center within yourself which can continue to regulate the expression of your energies.

The next chapter provides specific techniques which can help you to handle the conflicts of your t-square and build a center which can direct the multiplicity of selves within you. But before exploring these techniques, you can begin to expand your consciousness by viewing your t-square from several new perspectives. Intellect alone does not lead to understanding or facilitate lasting change. If you are to fully understand yourself and your vast possibilities, you must view yourself through many different lenses, including the lens of imagination or imagery.

Analogies

Overemphasizing your focal planet without attempting to integrate and balance the energies of all your planets is like starting your car by repeatedly pumping the accelerator. But racing your engine wastes gasoline, creates unnecessary noise and floods your carburetor, increasing your chances of catching on fire. Why burn out your psychological engine when you can maintain your physical and emotional health for

> *"Don't keep running your engine with a gasoline-soaked carburetor. Sooner than you expect you will catch on fire."*   MAX ALTH

years by conserving the fuel, available free of cost, from your natal planets?

A frequently used analogy for the t-square is a table with a missing leg, which is out of balance. Note that such a table leans upon the one leg which has no complement, but if pushed, topples in the direction of the missing leg. Collapsing in the direction of its weakness does not restore the balance of the table; nor does collapsing into your empty sign and house enable you to handle the energies of your t-square in a balanced manner. One of the most important lessons of the t-square is that you must develop the characteristics indicated by your empty space as constructively as possible, rather than retreat into their most negative expression when overemphasizing your focal planet destroys your equilibrium and wreaks havoc in your life.

Consider also a butterfly with a damaged or undeveloped wing, which is unable to fly. First, the undeveloped wing must grow or heal; then the butterfly must learn to use both wings, balancing them together. Likewise, you must learn not only to fly with both wings of your opposing planets, but also to grow a missing wing through cultivating the qualities indicated by the empty space in your t-square, coordinating them with the expression of your focal planet.

The planets in your natal chart also saunter and dance across the stage of your life in the manner of a troupe of marionettes, each dangling from strings manipulated by a puppeteer. The planets of your t-square may well be the main characters of the comedy or drama that you are performing in this incarnation, but they too are out of your control unless you, like the puppeteer, are able to rise above the show and direct its action. As long as you identify entirely with each of the marionettes, you are likely to feel helpless and to be entangled in the strings of your marionette personalities. Only by rising above the stage of your life and coordinating the movements of each of your personalities can you begin to enact the potential of your cosmic drama.

Another analogy appropriate to the t-square is that of a pendulum. A pendulum swings to the extreme right and extreme left when at the mercy of outside forces. In a like manner, you may experience your focal planet leading you first in one direction and then in another (often back and forth between your focal sign and house and your empty sign and house) without pausing in the middle. Consider how your life might be different if you were to control the fluctuations of your inner pendulum, allowing it to make smaller, less extreme arcs so that you might experience the benefits of directing your energies from a balanced center within yourself.

Consider also how the planets of your t-square pull you in three directions, much like you would be pulled if a rope were tied around your waist and one person pulled you forward, while two other people tugged in opposing directions upon each of your arms. How would you regain balance? Most likely, you would lean backward, but eventually your resistance would exhaust you and you would, in time, topple forward (in the direction of your focal planet).

Perhaps, if you knew how to collect and channel the vast reservoir of energy available to you, you might, like an expert in the martial arts, be able to draw energy from the outside forces pulling upon you, and to maintain a centered position indefinitely. But few people have, or can hope to develop, such powerful capabilities. Consider then what might happen if you were to give in to the pull of these conflicting forces, if you were to allow yourself to fall in the direction of your focal planet.

"Jung's method of therapy is designed to amplify rather than reduce the fault in the patient. Balance comes as a result of leaning on your faults."
JOSEPH CAMPBELL

166

The philosophy of Taoism is based upon the yin/yang duality, the interplay between two opposing energies in the universe, one regarded as feminine and receptive and the other as masculine and active. Since the nature of energy is to continually move and change, yin is continually becoming yang and yang becoming yin. Opposing energies lead to each other rather than apart. Likewise, astrologically, Aries leads to Libra, Taurus to Scorpio and each of the other signs to its opposing polarity. As opposing signs and houses intersect at the center of the chart, they also intersect and lead to you, at your position on earth at any given moment.

How does the above discussion relate to the phenomenon of falling into the focal area of your t-square by overemphasizing its characteristics? Consider, for example, what might happen if you were to express one sign in its extreme, totally ignoring the energies of the opposing sign. If you were to overemphasize the qualities of Capricorn by driving yourself to succeed and controlling your emotions so rigidly that you are unable to experience any fullness in your personal life, you would, if you were unhappy enough, begin to open yourself to Cancerian experiences of nourishment, nurturance and deep feeling. Likewise, expressing any of your planets and houses in an extreme manner would, in time, lead you to develop the opposite characteristics. By expressing your focal planet, sign and house fully, by giving into its pull upon you rather than attempting to maintain balance, you are eventually likely to swing full circle from the focal area of your t-square to the empty space. Hopefully then, you would not begin to fluctuate between these two facets of yourself, but would instead learn to integrate both, and to integrate all of your planets, signs and houses, by remaining aware of the needs of each one and directing their expression from your inner center, in attunement with your higher self.

HOW TO HANDLE YOUR T-SQUARE: TECHNIQUES

The techniques provided in this chapter can help you to understand your t-square, to become aware of alternate ways to express and channel its energies, and to experience these new alternatives, developing a center in yourself so that you can translate your awareness into constructive action.

These techniques are derived from: 1) my experience interpreting astrology charts; 2) study, training and practice in gestalt therapy, transactional analysis, psychosynthesis and meditation; 3) a lifetime of journal writing, and several years experience creating and teaching Journal Writing for Personal Growth; 4) two of my unpublished books, *The Book of Possibilities* (a workbook for discovering and actualizing one's "dreams") and *A Passing of Clouds* (a collection of personal insights).

This chapter is arranged according to techniques which can loosely be classified as astrological, introspective, dialoguing, meditative, creative and practical. If you have an air emphasis in your chart, a strong Mercury, or Virgo planets, the astrological and introspective techniques, which are analytical in nature, may appeal to you. If you have a fire emphasis or a prominent Sun, Mars or Moon, you may prefer the gestalt/dialogue or creative approaches which allow you to identify with different parts of yourself, experiencing them directly rather than analyzing them or detaching yourself from them.

If you have a water emphasis or a prominent Neptune, you may want to try meditative/intuitive techniques to disidentify with and transcend your emotional conflicts and to develop an inner center which can coor-

dinate all parts of your being; you may gravitate toward
directed fantasy or creative techniques which exercise
your imagination. If you have an earth emphasis or a
strong Saturn or Mercury, you may feel most comfortable
with practical techniques through which you can develop
concrete programs of action.

Beyond these techniques, you may choose to explore
some form of psychotherapy or personal/spiritual development which seems appropriate to you because its approach
harmonizes with an emphasis in your chart or the energies
of your focal planet; or you may, in contrast, pursue a
path which is more reflective of the planet, sign or
house of your empty space, and which helps you to express
these qualities.

The following table is a purely subjective classifi-
cation of therapies and related paths of development
according to the planets which are most expressive of
their approaches and techniques. Consider the signs and
houses ruled by these planets to also pertain to the
paths of development listed here.

WHICH PATH FOR YOU?

action therapy ♂♄	muscular therapy ♂♄♀
art therapy ☉♀♆	mysticism ♆♃
assertiveness training ♂☉	nutritional therapy ♀☽
astrology ♅☿	primal therapy ♀☽☉
behavior therapy ♂♄	psychiatry ☽♀♆
bibliotherapy ☿♃♄	psychoanalysis ☽♀♆♂
bioenergetics ♂♀	psychodrama ☉♂☽♆
client-centered therapy ☽♀♀	psychosynthesis ♆♃☉
directed fantasy ♆♃	rational-emot.therapy ☿♃
gestalt therapy ☉☽♂	reality therapy ☿♄♂
Jungian therapy ♆☽♀	Reichian therapy ♂♀
karate ♂♆♀	rolfing ♂♄♀
logotherapy ♃♆☊	t'ai chi chuan ♆♂
meditation ☿♆	transactional analysis ☿☽♄
movement therapy ♂☉♆	yoga ♂☉♆

169

Whatever approaches or techniques you use, they will help you only if you truly want to: a) expand your consciousness; b) develop constructive attitudes; c) practice new behaviors which can help you to resolve the problems created by your t-square; d) express your talents and strengths more fully; e) gain peace of mind.

Astrological Techniques

1. Become aware of all the positive manifestations of your focal planet according to its nature, its sign and its house. Focusing upon its positive characteristics will weaken the influence of its negative characteristics and enable you to function more effectively.

The preceding chapters on planets, signs and houses should help you understand what energies you need to cultivate. However, you must synthesize the meanings of the planet, sign and house, and discover how all three can operate together; you must also translate your understanding into effective action.

EXAMPLE: A woman with a focal Moon in Pisces in the 11th house is overly dependent upon her friends, sensitive to their reactions, and easily influenced by their opinions. She might need less from them if she moves into a house with other women, joins a spiritual or musical organization or actualizes her fantasy of becoming involved in the Big Sister program and befriending a disadvantaged girl.

2. Understand the empty space of your t-square and its most constructive manifestations. Consider all possible meanings of its sign and house, and how these might operate beneficially together. Determine which of these expressions of your empty space you want to develop. How might you develop them?

Because your empty space indicates "holes" in your personality, you may need to observe and interact with people who have an emphasis in this sign or house or who are strongly influenced by its ruler. From them you may gain awareness of qualities or areas of exper-

ience you have not developed, and may begin to learn
how developing this sign and house might benefit you.

*EXAMPLE: A man with a t-square to Sun in Capricorn in
the 6th house is dissatisfied because he must work two
jobs in order to pay off his debts and because he suf-
fers from ill health. His health might improve and he
might be happier if he expressed his Cancer in the 12th
house - taking better care of himself by preparing nourishing meals, and fulfilling his emotional needs by
forming deeper connections with his family or spending
his Sundays alone, relaxing by the water.*

3. Using Dane Rudhyar's *An Astrological Mandala* or Marc
   Edmund Jones' *The Sabian Symbols*, look up the Sabian
   Symbol for your empty space - the degree opposite your
   focal planet. (Always use the higher degree, unless
   the minutes are zero - e.g., use 17 degrees for 16 degrees 01 minutes and 16 degrees for 16 degrees 00 minutes.) If you have a focal planet conjunction, look up
   both degrees, as well as the degree for the midpoint
   between the two planets.

   Although the Sabian Symbol for the focal planet is
   probably important, the symbol for the empty space
   seems to be more significant. This symbol and its interpretation (vague, but highly evocative) usually
   provide a key to the deficiency indicated by the empty
   space, by suggesting the quality or approach which you
   need to develop. Reflect upon it; free associate. Consider what meaning it has in your life and what it can
   teach you.

   *EXAMPLE: A woman with a t-square to Mercury at 16 de-
   grees 18 minutes of Aries in the 6th house, with Mercury in exact square to Moon in Cancer in the 8th
   house, is fixated upon a marriage which ended five
   years ago. Rather than forming new relationships, she
   has been working compulsively ever since. The Sabian
   Symbol for her empty degree of 17 Libra is, according
   to Rudhyar, "A retired sea captain watches ships entering and leaving the harbor." His keynote interpretation reads: "the capacity to gain an objective and
   calm understanding of human experiences in which one
   was once deeply involved."*

171

4. Understand how you use the ruler of your empty sign according to the sign and house in which it is positioned in your chart. How might you apply its most positive expression to your empty space? Because you are used to experiencing and expressing this planet (unless, perhaps, the ruler is weakly positioned in your chart, or you haven't learned to channel its energies effectively), you have a clue to how you might develop your empty sign. Even if the ruler is involved in your t-square, you can learn from it if you have, at least upon occasion, used it beneficially. You might also try the same technique with the ruler of your empty house (e.g., Mars as ruler of the 1st house).

EXAMPLE: A woman with a t-square to Neptune in Libra in the 1st house easily absorbs the feelings of others and is overly compassionate; she is not able to assert her needs in close personal relationships. Mars, the ruler of her empty sign, is conjunct her Sagittarian Sun in the 3rd house. By understanding how she goes after what she wants and how she asserts herself in her daily interactions (after all, she functions well as a substitute teacher, and she drives somewhat aggressively to and from school), she might discover how to be more direct and assertive in her important relationships. (How? Just do it!)

5. Consider all of the possible ways in which you could constructively apply the energies of your focal planet and sign to your empty house (e.g., focal Jupiter in Cancer in the 8th house functioning as Jupiter in Cancer in the 2nd house) or express the energies of your focal planet in accordance with your empty sign and house (e.g., focal Jupiter in Cancer in the 8th house functioning as Jupiter in Capricorn in the 2nd house). Either of these techniques can help you to integrate your focal planet and empty space by creating a bridge between the two houses and signs. Only by becoming aware of new approaches to your experience and new patterns of behavior can you begin to actualize the potential of your t-square.

EXAMPLE: The woman in example 3, who has a t-square to Mercury in Aries in the 6th house, uses her empty space

*to reinforce the negative manifestations of her focal
planet. Dominating every conversation, she remains
totally oblivious to the other person. Repeatedly, she
discusses her past marriage and her psychological problems, particularly how isolated she feels working a-
lone seven days a week on projects she dislikes.*

*If she expressed her Mercury in Aries advantageously
in the 12th house, she might actively attempt to understand how her self-centeredness drives people away
or how she might make the work she does alone more fulfilling. Mercury expressed through Libra in the 12th
house could help her to cultivate inner balance so
that she works less compulsively, to objectively reflect upon her past marriage and learn from it, to focus upon current relationship issues, and to establish
new relationships of mutual benefit, in which she com-
municates her innermost thoughts but is also able to
please others, to respond to their needs and to help
them handle their personal relationships.*

6. A related way of understanding how you might integrate
   the expression of your focal planet and empty space is
   to imagine a conjunction occurring in your empty house
   between your focal planet and the ruler of your empty
   sign or house (e.g., focal Saturn in Taurus in the 4th
   house functioning as Saturn conjunct Pluto in Taurus
   or Scorpio in the 10th house). Understanding the meaning of such a conjunction, occurring in either your
   focal sign or empty sign, can enable you to discover
   new possibilities for developing your empty space in
   accordance with the energies of your focal planet.

   *EXAMPLE: A woman with a t-square to Venus in Virgo in
   the 9th house (with Venus ruling her Libran midheaven,
   and Saturn in Gemini in the 6th house opposing Moon
   in Sagittarius late in the 11th) has finally completed
   her Ph.D. in Mayan archaeology, but is unable to find
   employment either as an archaeologist or as a college
   professor. Imagining her Venus conjunct Neptune first
   in Virgo and then in Pisces led her to apply for a
   job planning the city museum's cultural programs, and
   to develop her photography skills so that she could
   sell photographs of Mexico to magazines.*

173

7. Reflect upon the positive expressions of each square and opposition in your t-square by considering how the planets, signs and houses involved in each aspect might cooperate together. The preceding chapters on opposing signs and houses should help you integrate your oppositions; you can apply the same principles to discovering ways to integrate opposing planets, as well as the planets, signs and houses involved in your squares.

Any aspect in your chart is a channel of energy between two of your planets; it may most often manifest in one particular manner, according to the nature of the aspect, but you can direct its energy to bring about a variety of other possible manifestations. Frequently, interpreting planets in square as if they are in trine or sextile (operating in the same signs and houses) and planets in opposition as if they are in conjunction (operating in either of the opposing signs and houses) can enable you to understand how the two planets can function harmoniously together. Once you gain this understanding, you can begin to express the combinations of planets, signs and houses involved in your squares and oppositions according to their highest possible manifestations.

EXAMPLE: A man has a t-square to Mercury in Scorpio in the 12th house, with Saturn in Leo in the 9th opposing Moon in Aquarius in the 3rd. Saturn and Mercury are in exact square. Berating himself for not fulfilling his father's expectations - for not developing any practical skills and for not getting into medical school, he works as an aide in a mental hospital and comes home each night, exhausted and depressed. If he were to use his Mercury/Saturn square as if it were a trine (perhaps operating from the early degrees of Leo to the late degrees of Scorpio) he might attempt to discover other work (possibly in a similar field) which is less psychologically draining. In his spare time, he might then be motivated to develop skills as a writer or researcher or to apply himself to a practical course of study which would enable him to fulfill his own expectations and feel less concerned about his father's expectations.

8. Another way to become aware of the potential of your squares and oppositions is to imagine the planets involved in these aspects positioned in each other's sign and house (e.g., Moon in Sagittarius in the 2nd house opposing Uranus in Gemini in the 8th might function as Moon in Gemini in the 8th opposing Uranus in Sagittarius in the 2nd). By exploring these possibilities, you begin to build a bridge between facets of yourself which have previously been in conflict.

EXAMPLE: A woman with a t-square to Uranus in Cancer in the 4th house has an opposition between Jupiter retrograde in Aries in the 12th (the focal planet of a bucket) and Saturn in Libra late in her 6th, conjunct the descendant. She is frequently torn between her desire to spend time alone (reading, reflecting and writing in her journal) and the responsibilities of both her job (which she dislikes, but which pays well) and a demanding love relationship.

Expressing Jupiter in her 6th and 7th houses, this woman has reduced her working hours to part-time so that she feels freer and less pressured. Having terminated a difficult relationship, she is now establishing looser but also more satisfying connections with other people. Expressing Saturn in her 12th house, she has used her spare time productively, completing a novella and spending months gaining knowledge about new employment opportunities.

She has decided that time to herself is her first priority, and worth having less money to spend. The keynote interpretation for her empty degree, according to Rudhyar, is "the will to unearth what has permanent value ... to let go of non-essentials."

9. Discover ways to synthesize the planets in your opposition and integrate them with your empty space by imagining how these two planets might function in conjunction together in the empty sign and house. How might they not only cooperate, but also help you to overcome the deficiencies of your empty space?

EXAMPLE: The woman described above is employed as a technician in a medical laboratory. Because her work

*does not fulfill her introspective and literary na-
ture, she is frequently besieged with feelings of
purposelessness; she releases the tension she experiences by moving or by changing laboratory jobs.*

*This woman is beginning to express Jupiter conjunct
Saturn in Capricorn in her empty 10th house by exploring possibilities for teaching creative writing
and dream interpretation to the elderly and by entering the publishing field as an apprentice to a
printer of poetry books.*

10. Study the meanings of the trines and sextiles, as
    well as the quintiles, to your t-square planets,
    particularly to your focal planet. Consider the
    planets, signs and houses involved in each aspect.
    How might these aspects provide constructive chan-
    nels for you to express the energy released by your
    t-square?

    *EXAMPLE: A woman with a t-square to Venus in Pisces
    in the 5th house has lost her job as an elementary
    school teacher and now allows the needs of her two
    daughters to dominate her life. Since she chauf-
    feurs them to dancing school every afternoon, she
    might activate her trine between focal Venus and
    Mars in Scorpio in the 1st house by enrolling in
    dance classes at the same time as them, actively
    and energetically expressing herself while also
    encouraging her daughters' self-expression.*

11. Although it may not aspect your t-square, the North
    Node can have a profound influence upon your over-
    all balance and harmony if you cultivate the quali-
    ties represented by its sign and house, and also by
    the position of its ruler in your chart. Developing
    your North Node is similar to developing your empty
    space; you feel deficient and somewhat insecure ex-
    pressing these energies, but the rewards of doing
    so are immeasurable. By becoming attuned to your
    North Node, you align yourself with the highest en-
    ergies of the universe, and are able to express the
    planets in your t-square and in the rest of your
    chart more constructively.

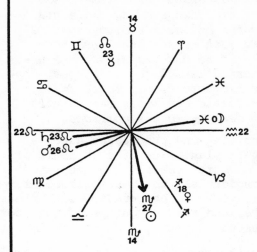

A CASE STUDY:
T-Square to Sun

Tom is a furniture maker who lives with his wife in the backwoods of Maine. His t-square to the Sun in Scorpio, his Mars/Saturn conjunction rising and six planets in fixed signs influence him to invest considerable energy in his work and to explode with frustration when problems arise. Usually, he vents his pent-up anger on his Piscean wife, accusing her of not responding to his needs, which in most cases he has not expressed. One source of Tom's conflicts is his inclination to hide away in his home, building extremely lavish and expensive pieces of furniture which few people in his area can afford, and which few know about because he has so little contact with the public.

If Tom were to integrate his Moon/Mars/Saturn opposition, he would remain in contact with his feelings, not only expressing his emotional needs on a daily basis, but also taking better care of himself and discovering constructive channels for releasing his frustration. He would invest more energy into strengthening his relationship with his wife, which has become shaky because of her highly sensitive responses to his temper. Expressing his focal Sun in Taurus in the 10th house, as well as his North Node, he would become more practical and more concerned with the financial resources and values of the public who might buy his work. The Sun's influence here would also motivate him to seek out potential customers and actively build his reputation, rather than wait for others to discover him. The Sabian Symbol for Tom's empty degree (27 Taurus) according to Rudhyar, is "an old Indian woman selling the artifacts of her tribe to passersby." The keynote interpretation is "peaceful adaptation to collective needs."

Currently, due to expenses resulting from the birth of their first child, Tom and his wife are moving near a large town and opening a small furniture shop. He has begun jogging every day to release tension, and is building smaller, more practical pieces of furniture in addition to the beautifully crafted but highly expensive cabinets which are his specialty.

177

EXAMPLE: A man with a t-square to Moon in Virgo in the 8th house has been divorced three times, each time because he spent his days reading while his wife worked and paid the bills. His South Node is in Sagittarius in the 12th house; his North Node, in Gemini in the 6th. If he had translated his understanding into practical skills by seeking employment in a writing or communication-related field, he might have prevented the conflicts represented by his t-square from destroying his marriages.

12. Remain aware of transiting and progressed aspects formed to your t-square planets and the channels of expression they provide for the tension generated by your t-square. Consider all the possibilities for expressing these influences in cooperation with the planets being aspects, and take advantage of the opportunities they present to you.

EXAMPLE: An editor with a t-square to Mercury in Gemini in the 2nd house has wanted to write a vocational self-help book, but has been unable to focus upon one project for any length of time. However, aware of transiting Pluto in her 6th trining her focal Mercury, she began her manuscript, and completed it under the pressure of transiting Saturn in Virgo in her 6th going stationary in square to focal Mercury.

Introspective Techniques

1. Review past experiences during which you expressed your focal planet, sign and house in a detrimental manner. What did you do? What motivated you? What did you gain or lose? What can you learn from these experiences? How can you avoid repeating them?

2. Review past experiences during which you expressed your focal planet, sign and house constructively. What did you do? What motivated you? How did you do it? What can you learn from each experience? How can you continue to express this planet constructively?

3. Consider the meaning of the empty space of your t-square. How and why do you avoid expressing it? Which of its characteristics make you uncomfortable? Why?

178

What do you tell yourself in order to avoid cultivating this sign or house? How could you change your attitude? Your actions?

4. Review past experiences during which you constructively expressed the sign and house of your empty space. How did you do it? What motivated you? How did you feel? What did you gain? What can you learn from these experiences? How can you continue to develop and express this sign and house constructively?

5. Review past experiences during which you positively or negatively expressed: a)other t-square planets b)t-square oppositions and squares c)sextiles and trines to your t-square d)progressed and transiting aspects to your t-square e)aspects formed by planets of other people in your life. As with your focal planet and empty space, ask yourself how and why you acted or reacted as you did, and how you can express these energies to your own advantage.

Dialoguing Techniques

1. Either orally or in writing, create a dialogue between: a)opposing planets in your t-square b)your focal planet and a planet which it squares c)your focal planet and the ruler of your empty sign d)a t-square planet and a natal planet which sextiles or trines it e)a t-square planet and another person's planet which aspects it f)a t-square planet and a transiting/progressed planet currently aspecting it.

(These dialogue techniques are extremely powerful. Not only can they help you to understand how your planets operate in relationship to each other, they can also enable you, experientially, to integrate their conflicting energies. You must, however, become emotionally involved in the dialogue, identifying with each of the planets concerned and expressing yourself from that planet's point of view.

At first you may want to familiarize yourself with the above techniques and those which follow by creating dialogues between planets, signs *or* houses rather than

179

GESTALT THERAPY AND ASTROLOGY

Gestalt therapy, a relatively new form of psychotherapy developed by Fritz Perls, teaches us that we can make peace with ourselves if we are willing to own and fully experience those parts of ourselves a) which continually battle with each other b) which we deny and repress, and c) which we project outwardly onto other people or our environment. In order to help us integrate the opposing forces within us, gestalt therapists suggest that we use a technique similar to psychodrama, which involves personifying two different "personalities" which are at odds within us, and bringing them into relationship with each other through dialogue. Each "personality" must confront, listen to and accept the other before either one is willing to compromise and before both are capable of functioning together.

Gestalt therapy is compatible with astrology because its view of the process leading from inner conflict to self-integration is similar in meaning to two related cycles in astrology - that of the moon, from new to full to new again, and that of planetary aspects in general, from conjunction to opposition to conjunction. But not only can we understand our oppositions and conjunctions in terms of gestalt therapy theory, we can also use gestalt therapy techniques to resolve the inner conflicts represented by oppositions, and to a lesser extent, squares in our charts. When we are able to turn an opposition into a conjunction, or a square into a trine, we are able to resolve the conflict represented by that square or opposition.

...According to gestalt therapy, most of us are incapable of experiencing the polarities or contradictions within us for any length of time. When we feel in conflict between two parts of ourselves (such as our work responsibilities and our desire to relax and take it easy) we tend to identify with one and project the other outward, so that we perceive it as an alien force infringing upon our happiness. Once perceived as an external force (such as "the Job" or "the Boss"), we feel helpless, and unable to do anything except squirm under the oppression of something or someone other than ourselves. Only when we own our projections (such as by affirming, "I want work which is challenging") are we able to gain any power in our lives.

Another method of coping with inner conflict is repression. Often, when we judge a particular behavior or emotion as negative, we refuse to come to terms with it in ourselves. We push it aside, pretending that it doesn't exist. But denying it does not get rid of it; rather, denial forces the behavior or emotion to operate subconsciously, distorting our original motives or bursting through our consciousness when our guard is down and taking control over our actions. We then become compulsive. We do not know why we are acting as we do, and we feel as if we are possessed by an alien force.

A third way of coping with internal contradiction is introjection. When we introject something, we swallow it whole without digesting it. Common introjects are the explicit or implicit rules of our parents or peer group, which we often phrase as "I should..." But most "I should's" are "You should's" in disguise - voices of people of the past or present whom we feel we must please in order to feel all right about ourselves. Because a "You should" feels alien, our psyche often rejects it or rebels against it. "You should lose weight" leads to an ice cream splurge; "you should be working" leads to a day wasted in front of the television set.

In gestalt therapy, the splitting of our consciousness into two parts at war with each other is referred to as the battle between Topdog and Underdog. Topdog is the part of ourselves which tries to boss us around. It is often a conglomeration of parental advice about how we should be. Underdog is the part of ourselves which defends us against Topdog with such protests as "I don't want to," "I'm tired," and "Leave me alone." Underdog begs, cajoles, makes excuses, rebels. In most battles, Underdog wins because he has mastered the art of getting his own way. He simply refuses to cooperate. Since he is a powerful part of ourselves and not an introject, Topdog cannot act without him.

When Underdog wins the battle with Topdog, we enjoy ourselves immensely but our lives become chaotic. We neglect our responsibilities; we indulge ourselves by giving in to every whim without thinking of the consequences; we lose the approval of the people who are important to us, and our own self esteem; we feel guilty. When Topdog wins (and he wins only by gaining Underdog's grudging and usually temporary cooperation), we behave as we should behave. We work hard; we are polite; we do everything that would please mommy and daddy and establish ourselves as respected members of the community. But after awhile we begin to feel empty and depressed. We are doing the "right" things, but they don't seem right because they don't leave us with any feelings of satisfaction.

The battle between Topdog and Underdog can be characterized in a variety of ways, among them: a)I should vs. I want b)duty vs. pleasure c)reason vs. instinct d)desire for approval vs. desire to have our own way e)strength vs. weakness f)society vs. self g)independence vs. dependence h)self-sufficiency vs. helplessness, and i)productivity vs. laziness. Generally, Topdog and Underdog are two extremes of ourselves, neither one of them functional in daily living. At war with each other, they become exaggerated and distorted. They are like two people living in the same house, refusing to listen to each other, but each trying to gain control over the household. When Topdog becomes the stern father, Underdog becomes the wayward child. The more Topdog demands, the more Underdog resists. Neither of them gives an inch...No sooner does one get his way for any length of time then the other demands to be heard and fights for control. We seesaw back and forth between overly rational behavior and irrational behavior, between inhibition and extravagance.

How then do we get out of this dilemma? The resolution lies not in following the path of Topdog or Underdog, but in experiencing both of them fully and bringing them into contact until they are willing to listen to each other and agree upon one course of action. When this happens, both Topdog and Underdog disappear, and a new voice emerges which is unconflicted and unopposed. This new voice is partially an assimilation of both Topdog and Underdog; it has accepted certain qualities of each and rejected others. But it is more than an assimilation, because it has developed apart from Topdog and Underdog and is open to new ways of thinking and acting. When this voice emerges, we are no longer chained to the repetitive cycles of the past; we are free to move on, experiencing unity in ourselves.

But exactly how, we may ask, does gestalt therapy help us to bring Topdog and Underdog together so that we no longer seesaw between extremes in ourselves? Its primary technique is that of identifying with both Topdog and Underdog, bringing them into contact with each other by creating a dialogue between them. We become Topdog and tell Underdog what we think of him and how he should be; then we become Underdog and defend ourselves - making excuses, yelling, crying, calling Topdog names, or whatever other way we have of dealing with his perpetual tyrannizing. Then we become Topdog again and shuttle back and forth between the two until we reach a resolution or an impasse. If indeed we do become stuck, and are more aware of the chasm between the two than ever before, we may feel blank for awhile - helpless, paralyzed, exhausted. When this happens, we may want to quit and resume the dialogue at a later date when we have had time to assimilate the energies that have emerged within us. Just because we do not reach a resolution immediately does not mean that we have not benefited from the process. Rather, by identifying fully with each part of ourselves and bringing them into relationship, we are beginning to build a bridge which will eventually link the two together.

One way of dealing with an impasse in the dialogue is, of course, to quit. Another way is to allow ourselves to fully experience the impasse. In gestalt therapy, this impasse or blankness is not considered to be a dead end, but rather to be a fertile void. From this void, the new voice will eventually emerge, but not until Topdog and Underdog have expressed themselves fully and forcefully. Mere verbiage will not do; we must be emotionally involved in the process; we must identify with each one so completely that we shake with anger or collapse into tears. If we are in a group or with a therapist or friend, we may become more involved in the dialogue than if we are alone, for the presence of supportive persons encourages us to go further than we might go by ourselves. But we can still become emotionally invested in the dialogue when alone, talking aloud to ourselves or writing in a journal.

Whatever setting we choose, as long as we persevere and re-enact the dialogue from time to time, a new voice is likely to emerge. Whether in the fertile void or during the actual conversation between opposing energies, we experience then a moment of illumination, a change in consciousness. At that moment, we transcend the conflict between Topdog and Underdog; we discover an alternative way of being.

...Now that we understand the process of gestalt therapy dialogue, how do we go about applying it to an astrological context? First, we study our charts and select an opposition or square which we can understand in terms of our personal conflicts. We might at this time take a few minutes to study this aspect objectively, to understand its astrological meaning, and to reflect upon the specific ways we experience it in our lives. If we experience the opposition or square most obviously in terms of its planets, its signs or its houses, we would start with only one of these three variables (e.g. Mars opposition Venus, apart from their sign and house placements), rather than all three together.

Once we are oriented to the meaning of the aspect, we are ready to begin the dialogue. First, we identify with one of the planets (and/or its sign or house). As that planet, we talk or write in the first person about how we feel and what we want. Then we identify with the second planet, describing how we feel and what we want from the point of view of that planet. Next, as the first planet again, we respond to the second, telling it what we think or feel about what it has just said. The second planet in turn responds to the first, and so on until we can go no further. While the dialogue is in process, we must put our astrological knowledge aside and let each planet speak spontaneously, even if it is not being true to its astrological meaning. Astrology has helped us to define and focus upon a specific conflict; our organisms must now experience it fully and discover a possible resolution.

...When we feel finished, we can benefit by reflecting upon what has happened. We can define the conflict clearly. Then we can ask ourselves how we can reach a compromise or synthesis between the opposing energies, even if only a temporary one. If we are really stuck and cannot discover a possible resolution, we can turn back to astrology and analyze how these two planets might function harmoniously together.

attempting to experience the complexity of planet, sign *and* house positions interacting together. You may discover that by identifying with a planet, you subconsciously express its sign and house, or by identifying with a sign or house, you experience the energies of the planet. The following pages describe the purpose of this dialoguing process and how you can use it in coordination with your chart. The dialogues and dramatizations in the last chapter of this book reveal how the above techniques and other techniques included in this section can: a)awaken your creativity b)allow you to experience the disparate parts of yourself and bring them into contact with each other c)begin to resolve the conflicts in your life and fulfill the potential of your birthchart.)

EXAMPLE: A woman with a t-square to Mars in Aries in the 5th house fluctuates dramatically between her 2nd house Capricorn Sun and her 8th house Cancer Moon. One year, she drives herself relentlessly in order to succeed at sales work, avoiding any emotional entanglements and refusing financial help from her wealthy mother; the next year, she quits her job, engages in numerous affairs, and cultivates her relationship with her mother, from whom she now accepts lavish gifts.

"I want to be self-sufficient," her Sun tells her Moon. "You're too dependent." Her Moon responds, "Stop trying to deprive me! I want to be loved. And why should I work when mother sends me money?" After conducting several Sun/Moon dialogues, this woman begins to realize that she can work and accept occasional help from her mother without becoming overly dependent, and that she can derive satisfaction from relationships without maintaining an all-or-nothing approach to love.

2. Either orally or in writing, dialogue with your focal planet. Express how you feel about it. Tell it about the problems it has created for you, and how it has, and how it can, benefit you. Ask it what it wants and what it needs and why it is or is not satisfied. Allow your planet to respond and to enlighten you about the role it plays in your life. Dialogue also with the ruler of your empty sign or house, and with other planets in or outside of your t-square.

*EXAMPLE: A Sagittarian with an 11th house emphasis and
a t-square to Neptune in Libra in the 9th house continually drifts from one spiritual movement to the
next. Disillusioned with one, he becomes a dedicated
follower in another until he experiences the same dis-
illusionment. In a counselling session, he conducted
the following dialogue with Neptune:*

CLIENT: *You keep disappointing me. You give so much
    meaning to my life. I get so high, and then you pull
    the rug out from under me.*
NEPTUNE: *You trust people too easily. You want to be
    enlightened but you want them to do it for you.*
CLIENT: *What do you want me to do?*
NEPTUNE: *Meditate more often. In groups, you get high
    on other people's energy, not your own.*
CLIENT: *What do you need?*
NEPTUNE: *I need to be heard.*
CLIENT: *How can I hear you?*
NEPTUNE: *Listen. I'm always here.*
CLIENT: *Who are you?*
NEPTUNE: *I'm your inner guide.*
CLIENT: *Are you telling me I should stop going to the
    spiritual center, and just meditate on my own?*
NEPTUNE: *No. But don't expect them to give you what
    I can give you. I have what you're looking for, but
    you don't want to hear it.*
CLIENT: *Why don't I want to hear it?*
NEPTUNE: *Because you won't need to go to the spiritual
    center, and if you don't go, you'll lose the friends
    that you have there.*

*Once this man acknowledged his desire to associate
with spiritually-oriented people, he continued to join
spiritual groups, but without deluding himself that
they would enlighten him. He also meditated more often.*

3. Begin a dialogue between two planets in your t-square
   and gradually bring several of your other planets into
   the conversation, as if you are conducting a town meeting attended by your "subpersonalities." Most likely,
   your focal planet will be the self-proclaimed chairman,
   and will dominate the meeting. Let him speak to your
   other planets, but allow them to respond, expressing
   their needs and their reactions. Select an important

conflict in your life, and discover if your planets can agree upon a course of action which enables you to function as a whole rather than as a conglomeration of disassociated parts.

EXAMPLE: See the opening dialogue in the last chapter. (But you need not write a story. Simply dialogue.)

4. With friends, family or other astrology students, enact your t-square or your entire chart. Choose, or let your actors choose their roles, describing each planet briefly so that they understand how you experience it. You may want to participate (perhaps as your focal planet) or you may instead stand back and observe your psyche in action. As the theme of your drama (or comedy), choose an issue related to your t-square, one that is particularly relevant to you now.

EXAMPLE: A woman with a t-square to a 6th house Moon might dramatize her conflicts about leaving a secure and comfortable job for a challenging new position.

Meditative Techniques

1. Rather than dialogue aloud or on paper, allow yourself to relax by meditating for a few minutes, and then fantasize an encounter with one of your t-square planets or with the ruler of your empty space. Let the planet emerge of its own accord; it may appear as a "subpersonality" in its own right - perhaps as a lonely child if Moon in Capricorn, a bullfighter if Mars in Taurus, or a princess if Venus in Leo. Ask what it needs, what it wants and what it can teach you, and listen carefully to its response. You might also allow it to present you a gift before departing.

EXAMPLE: A woman with a t-square to Venus in Gemini in the 7th house conducted a fantasy dialogue with a butterfly. "I want to be free to fly," the butterfly told her. "I need space to spread my wings...I can teach you to drink nectar from a flower without being trapped by its petals." The gift the butterfly gave was one of her antennae. Her parting words were: "Use this to help you select the right flower."

2. Meditate upon the Sabian Symbol for your focal planet or empty degree, visualizing the image associated with it. (Reading and free-associating from Rudhyar's interpretation in *An Astrological Mandala* may help you to become attuned to its meaning.) Allow it to emerge on its own and to reveal to you the lessons of your focal planet or empty degree.

   EXAMPLE: The woman in the previous example, with a t-square involving Moon in Pisces in the 4th opposing Saturn in Virgo in the 10th, both squaring Venus in Gemini in the 7th, claims that she is eager to marry. However, torn between hunger for love and fear of closeness, she becomes involved in brief, superficial relationships in which she allows unusual drug-related sexual experiences (Neptune in exact trine to Venus) to substitute for real intimacy. The Sabian Symbol for her Venus is: "In a Northern village, men cut the ice of a frozen pond during winter...the farsighted use of natural resources to supply future needs." This woman could easily meditate upon a frozen pond, but she could not visualize the cutting of the ice without a flood of tears. Allowing herself to cry while meditating upon this image, she began to acknowledge the deepseated needs she had been denying, and to realize that if she actually wanted a serious relationship, she would have to experience those needs and risk sharing them with others.

3. Meditate upon your focal planet, your empty sign and house or your focal planet applied to your empty sign and house, allowing images to surface which represent these facets of your chart. If no images emerge, develop your own and meditate upon them, or begin with one of the planetary images on the following page. Use an image associated only with a planet or one that also incorporates its sign and house.

   EXAMPLES:
   Pluto in Cancer in the 5th house- a skindiver painting an underwater mural
   Pluto applied to Capricorn in the 11th house- an archaeologist uncovering artifacts of human society on a mountain top
   Moon in Sagittarius in the 2nd house- a blanket cover-

PLANETARY IMAGES

SUN- king, noble, president, central government, movie star, rooster, aorta, solar plexus, fulcrum, hearth, main street, stage, conductor, director, landlord

MOON- blanket, wool, snail, pouch, swamp, oven, womb, egg, basket, hammock, pitcher, milk, kitchen, tides, fruit, sponge, octopus, cottage, well, robe, canoe

MERCURY- transmitter, telegraph, telephone, answering machine, marketplace, ant hill, microscope, grater, chain link, centipede, chameleon, capillary, bridge, fly, conjunction, salad, parrot, carrier pigeon

VENUS- magnet, honey, flower, sugar, cream, perfume, satin, duet, accompaniment, chorus, wedding, oil & vinegar, scale, garden, venus flytrap, butterfly, dove, park, rainbow, vein, harem, princess

MARS- automobile, truck, engine, accelerator, green light, artery, open door, amplifier, gun, warrior, gladiator, athlete, sword, match, fuel, dynamite, fire, hounds, serpent, bugle, military band, flag

JUPITER- caretaker, benefactor, guardian angel, nomad, trail, sunflower, escalator, telescope, magic carpet, prophet, cornucopia, banquet, Santa Claus, balloon, giraffe, clown, parade, roller coaster, suburbs

SATURN- building, foundation, fortress, mountain, rock, fence, filter, wall, cement, closet, anchor, iceberg, shellfish, red light, island, backbone, lock, brakes, watchdog, desert, tree, check, weeping willow

URANUS- lightning, electricity, sparkler, live wire, albatross, rare animal, hermaphrodite, dwarf, gypsy, tornado, earthquake, tympani, comet, rocket, meteor, explosion, exclamation point, eggplant, black sheep

NEPTUNE- fog, mist, mirage, cloud, smokescreen, vapor, silhouette, masquerade, prism, mirror, unicorn, silk, wave, candle, sieve, sheep, guerrilla, sniper, harp, trance, parentheses, labyrinth, crystal ball, soap bubble, dolphin, grail, ferris wheel

PLUTO- x-ray, buried treasure, volcano, black lights, wasp, bass, shadow, deepsea diver, reservoir, bomb, sewer, dungeon, basement, pipeline, tunnel, gorge, excavation, furnace, cemetery, ouija board, dragon, demon, phoenix, undergrowth, lava, midnight

ing a hope chest
Moon in Gemini in the 8th house- a covered passageway linking a bank and a psychologist's office
Mercury in Aries in the 10th house- a fly darting across the ceiling
Mercury in Libra in the 4th house- two flies meeting on the floor of a room

NOTE: You might also try this technique with images for your opposing planets operating in conjunction or expressing themselves in each other's sign and house. ("*In order to attain this union...of opposites...the alchemists tried not only to visualize the opposites together but to express them in the same breath" JUNG)*

4. Once you understand the positive expression of your focal planet, squares, oppositions, empty space and trines and sextiles, you can begin to visualize yourself expressing these energies. These visualizations, incorporated into your meditations, will not only increase your desire to manifest new traits, but will bring about the physical condition you envision.

5. Develop a mantra related to the positive expression of your focal planet in the empty space or the empty space itself. Be sure to word it positively (i.e. "I am humanity; humanity is me" for Aries in the 11th house rather than "I am not alone"). You may want to use an inspirational quotation, not only repeating it to yourself throughout the day but also posting it on the wall. If your empty space is the 7th house, develop a mantra related to your expression, not another person's expression, of its sign or planet.

EXAMPLES:
Capricorn in the 2nd house- "To sustain life we need less rather than more." (THOREAU)
Virgo in the 1st house- "The gods help him who helps himself." (EURIPIDES)
Aquarius in the 9th house- "And ye shall seek the truth and the truth shall make ye free." (ST. JOHN)
Sagittarius in the 11th house- "'Tis not too late to seek a newer world" (TENNYSON)
Capricorn in the 12th house- "I am the captain of my soul." (HENLEY)

Pisces in the 3rd house- "Live the ideal life right
  now." (MILLER)
Sagittarius in the 7th house- "Where you do not find
  love put love and there you will find it."(ST.JOHN)
Aries in the 12th house- "The happiest of all lives
  is a busy solitude."
Sagittarius in the 5th house- "Explore your own heart
  for there are both Rama and Allah." (KABIR)
Taurus in the 11th house- "The only way to have a
  friend is to be one."
Leo in the 1st house- "Be ye lamps unto yourselves."
  (UPANISHADS)
Capricorn in the 1st house- "The world will be com-
  plete for him who is himself complete." (MILLER)

6. Ask the *I Ching*, tarot, runes or Astro-Dice about
   issues related to your t-square (e.g. *How can I best
   express my focal planet? What can I learn from my t-
   square?)* and reflect upon the response you receive,
   listening to your own intuition. Keep a notebook of
   your questions, responses and free associations.

Creative Techniques

1. LATERAL THINKING: Develop your creative thinking by
   brainstorming images which express your squares or
   oppositions. These images can be used in dialoguing,
   meditation and writing, and are powerful personal
   archetypes that can inspire creative projects.

   EXAMPLE: *Images for my own Moon/Uranus square: gypsy
   tent, emancipated snail, bursting water pipe, hurri-
   cane, home hit by tornado, black sheep feeding, crazy
   quilt, automated kitchen, tribe of wild indians, (electric) incubator, electric blanket, broken/exploding
   egg, home computer, fountain of fireworks, beatnik
   landlady, kangaroo's pouch, house of the 7 dwarves.*

2. WRITING: The planets in your t-square are your best
   source of characters for stories and plays. Begin to
   know them by keeping a journal in which you write
   about them and/or engage in dialogue with them. Allow
   them to speak in the 1st person, so that you can begin to identify with their energies.

3. WRITING: Determine the theme of your t-square in rela-

tion to the dramas of your focal planet, and write
a fairy tale based upon it. Or, write a story with
characters representing your t-square planets, or a
play in which your t-square planets dialogue. Allow
the plot, theme, conflict and resolution to evolve
from your own life; do not force it into any prede-
termined pattern. (Considering the characters, plots
and themes of your favorite novels, plays or films
can help you discover appropriate story lines). Such
writing may not only be highly creative and powerful;
it may also transform you.

*EXAMPLE: The Wizard of Oz, Close Encounters of the
Third Kind and A Thousand Clowns relate to the planets in my t-square(p.195) and have helped me develop
creative writing ideas. Two fairy tales I have written express my t-square planets - one about a girl
who had to be different, and another about a princess who ran away to live with an "ideal" family,
and earned her right to stay by being of service to
an eccentric gnome. Writing the last chapter of this
book, which is not exactly a story, was by far my
most illuminating writing experience.*

4. ART: To facilitate the creative process, use your
   left hand (or right hand if you are lefthanded) to
   draw your impression of your t-square planets, empty
   space, or t-square as a whole. Use whatever colors
   seem appropriate. Pay attention to the feelings that
   emerge as you draw. You might also draw images related to your Sabian Symbols or t-square meditations.
   Aim for free-flowing creativity; you can develop a
   finished product later. (Drawings in response to such
   questions as *Where have I been? Where am I now? Where
   am I going? What is blocking me?* may also be helpful.)
   Verbalizing what each drawing means to you will enable you to gain insight about the energies expressed.

5. MUSIC: Reflect upon your favorite songs. Which ones
   express your t-square? What songs represent your empty space? Write a song or develop a piece of music
   related to your t-square planets. (*Recent Advances
   in Natal Astrology,* compiled by Geoffrey Dean, discusses the correlations of planets, signs and degrees
   with musical instruments and musical notes.)

Practical Techniques

1. Develop a plan of action oriented toward expressing the potential of your t-square. Determine your goal, and small, realistic tasks (that each of your planets agree to) which you can fulfill on a regular basis. Deal with resistances that emerge, and revise your plan accordingly. Reward yourself for your progress.

2. Keep a "credit log" in which you briefly record each experience in which you express your t-square constructively.

3. Experiment with *acting as if* you have resolved the dilemmas of your t-square, by attempting new behaviors in carefully selected situations. Such behaviors might seem artificial at first, but with time and practice, may become spontaneous.

4. Attend to any imbalance in your body chemistry by eating foods and taking vitamins, minerals and cell salts related to the sign, house or ruler of your empty space. (See *Astrology, Nutrition and Health* by Robert Jansky). If the empty space is the 1st or 6th house, if it is ruled by planets tenanting your 1st or 6th house, or co-ruled by your ascendant ruler, many of your conflicts may be related to or magnified by nutritional deficiencies.

5. No activity is likely to be as conducive to resolving the dilemmas of your t-square as singleminded commitment to a practical ideal. The process of applying yourself to a task agreed to by all your planets can awaken your center or Self, enabling you to balance and direct the energies of your t-square.

- - - - -

NOTE REGARDING THE FOLLOWING CHAPTER:
"Becoming Whole" was written in 1979, when Saturn was crossing my Venus/Saturn conjunction in Virgo, and I was struggling with experiences of isolation and alienation. Now in 1986, I hesitate to present myself in terms of an earlier self which I have outgrown; I feel compelled to add that the process of encountering my t-square planets in the writing of this chapter transformed the psychodynamics of my t-square, and therefore of my experience of myself and the world. The result - new sources of fulfillment, and of course, new conflicts to resolve!

BECOMING WHOLE

My t-square family is battling. This time, Moon in Aries, rather than Uranus, sparks the quarrel. "You promised me!" she screams, nearly falling off her perch on the nadir. "I would never have helped write one book for six months and neglected my other activities if you hadn't promised me that I could tell ALL about myself in the last chapter!"

Neptune in the 10th, who opposes Moon, cringes. "But you'd expose everything," she murmurs tearfully. "I could never face a single reader if you had your way."

Sun in Libra in the 9th, also opposing Moon, sides with Neptune. "Of course, we'll let you express yourself," she soothes Moon before adopting another point of view. "But this isn't a book about you. We have to consider the needs of all of us and satisfy our readers. Now if we shared the wisdom we've gained from our relationships..."

"WISDOM FROM RELATIONSHIPS! PHOOEY!" interrupts Uranus in Cancer in the 7th, who squares them all and is fidgety from being contained between the pages of a book for half a year and being deprived of any social stimulation outside her natal family. "You all don't know the first thing about wisdom! Moon wants to talk about herself and Sun wants to express the understanding she's gained with other people and Neptune wants to fantasize about the ideals she's fulfilling without taking any emotional risks. I run this family, not any of you, and I say that if we're going to talk about ourselves and our relationships, we have to tap higher levels and impart universal truths that have relevance to everyone."

Uranus reaches for her electronic tommy gun, ready to zap each of the other planets so that she can run out looking for excitement while they sleep, but Sun in Libra grabs her hand and pats it reassuringly. "Uranus," she smiles. "There's no need to quarrel. We can cooperate. We're all concerned with our own truths, whether personal or impersonal, and with what we've learned living together and relating to other natal families."

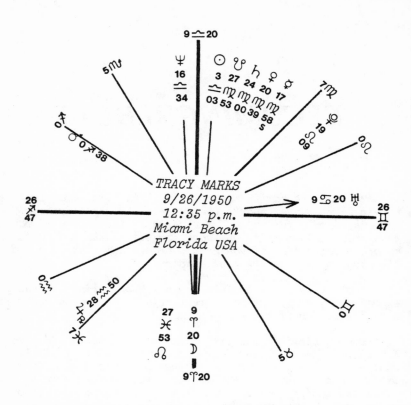

ASPECTS WITHIN T-SQUARE

aspect		orb
☽ ☌ IC	☽ ☍ MC	exact
☽ □ ♅		exact
♅ □ MC	♅ □ IC	exact
☉ ☍ ☽	☉ ☌ MC	6-17
☉ □ ♅		6-17
♆ ☍ ☽	♆ ☌ MC	7-14
♆ □ ♅		7-14

DIRECT MIDPOINTS

midpoint		orb
♅ = ☽ MC		exact
☉ = ♅ asc.		exact
MC = ☉ ♆	☽ = ☉ ♆	0-29
MC = ♂ ♅	☽ = ♂ ♅	0-33
☉ = MC ☊	☉ = ♀ ♆	0-33
☉ = ♀ ♆		0-47
☉ = ♄ MC		1-23

MAJOR ASPECTS TO T-SQUARE

aspect	orb
☉ ✳ ♂	2-25
♆ ✳ ♂	2-35
☉ ☌ ♅	5-10
☉ □ asc.	6-16
☽ △ ♂	8-42
☉ ☌ ♄	9-03

MINOR ASPECTS TO T-SQUARE

♅ quintile ♀
♅ quintile ♄   (wide)
♅ biquintile ♂
♆ semisextile ☿
♆ semisquare ♂
☉ semisquare ♀
☉ inconjunct ♃   (wide)
☽ novile ♃
♅ novile & parallel ♀
♆ contraparallel ♀

total lunar eclipse 9/26 **3♈**   solar eclipse 9/12 **18♍**

"And we want to inspire and help people," volunteers Neptune. *"Even Moon can draw from the waters beneath the nadir. Even she's attuned to the collective unconscious."*

"I want to talk about me!" asserts Moon.

"We need help," declares Sun in Libra, eyeing Moon warily and wondering if the book will ever be ready for publication. *"Neptune, call my home, the 9th house. Ring up your semisextile to my roommate, Mercury in Virgo, and tell him we're all coming over. After all, he's writing this book, and he should be able to analyze the situation and discover a solution acceptable to all of us."*

Mercury is sitting stationary, as usual, in his chair, reading and writing when his relatives arrive. Squared by transiting Neptune, he gazes up at them bleary-eyed, through a fog of inspiration.

"I've been assessing this family conflict," ponders Mercury, *"And I notice that Moon in Aries has been quiet for many months, and deserves to have her say, provided that she respects Neptune's sensitivity and allows each of you to express yourself in your own way. But before you arrived,"* Mercury continues, *"I was reading Hermann Hesse. He once wrote a message which relates to all of us. He speaks with Moon's candor and Uranus' and Sun's dedication to understanding and truth and Neptune's inspiration and idealism. If we read it together and acknowledge our common purpose, the rest of the book will follow. Transiting Saturn, who's conjuncting me at the moment, is determined to complete it."*

"Let's read it," urges Moon in Aries. *"Let's begin!"*

Mercury passes the book from hand to hand:

MOON IN ARIES:	*"I am*
NEPTUNE:	*a poet,*
SUN IN 9TH:	*a seeker,*
MOON IN ARIES:	*and a confessor,*
URANUS:	*obligated to truth*
MOON IN ARIES:	*and sincerity.*
NEPTUNE IN 10th:	*I have a mission,*
MERCURY/SATURN:	*albeit small and confined:*
NEPTUNE IN 10TH:	*to help other seekers*
SUN IN 9TH:	*to understand and cope with the world*
ALL TOGETHER:	*if only by assuring them*
	that they are not alone."

195

I have not mastered my t-square. Each day, I struggle to maintain order in my planetary household, as Uranus in Cancer in the 7th house pulls me off center, insisting upon following her own path apart from the other planetary members, and searching continually for new sources of stimulation; as Sun in Libra in the 9th house beckons me to open the attic windows of my psyche and behold the highest realms of understanding, all the while yearning for relationships based upon that common understanding, and shying away from discord and the casual exchanges of daily interactions; as Moon in Aries on the nadir endows each experience with a fanfare of enthusiasm, and hurls herself precariously into new adventures, attempting to meet her needs in as candid and forthright a manner as possible, while refusing to budge from the protection of home; as Neptune in Libra in the 10th house overreacts with painful sensitivity to every situation and person, but remains illuminated by her vision and dedicates herself with faith and inspiration to actualizing her ideals.

No, I have not mastered my t-square. If I look to other people to assess how they handle similar conflicts, I easily despair, for they, more likely than not, are far ahead of me in regard to my own issues, although they may be striving awkwardly and hesitantly to resolve issues of their own. If I converse with the Self that begins to emerge in me, that represents all that I am longing to become, I feel at times small and insignificant, because she is so wise, so incomparably more unified and beautiful than I. But if I play back the reels of my life and view how I have progressed in ten years time, how my planetary selves have begun to acknowledge, accept and encourage each other, even upon occasion to treat each other with respect and tenderness, I am awed by the capacity of a human being to change and grow and transform oneself despite apparently insurmountable odds.

I have what most astrologers would regard to be a difficult chart - a t-square, no trines within allowable orbs, and only two sextiles(one of them the nearly universal Neptune sextile Pluto). My t-square is particularly strong not only because it occurs on the angles and involves a full moon opposition (on the wake of an eclipse), four planets instead of three, and an exact square, but also because the midpoint of Sun and Neptune is my midheaven, forming an opposition with a 28 minute orb to my Moon, and a square with the same orb to focal Uranus. In addition to being imbued with the oversensitivity and idealism of Sun/Neptune, my midheaven and Moon are also my Mars/Pluto midpoint, and are therefore a channel for the release of powerful energies.

My chart is contradictory. "Why," I have sometimes asked myself, "If I had to be born a Libra, must I also have a t-square to the 7th house, which does not easily allow me to establish satisfying relationships? Why, if my t-square must be to the 7th house, must the focal planet be Uranus, who is totally at odds with the security needs of my Venus/Saturn conjunction and my Moon on the nadir? Why, with Moon on the nadir desiring to retreat into the warm comforts of the womb, must it exactly square Uranus in *Cancer*, who continually generates tidal waves to provoke the Moon out of hiding? Why must the Moon's needs be denied by an eclipse, which cuts it off from the sources of its own nourishment?"

"Why," I have asked, "With Capricorn as the empty sign of my t-square, must it be extraordinarily difficult to develop, by virtue of being intercepted? Why does its ruler Saturn conjunct the South Node, so that each time I express Saturnian or Capricornian energies, I am directed away from the North Node which is my life task? Why, if Mars is the natural ruler of my empty house, must it defy expression by operating subliminally in the 12th house, and by often compulsively and uncontrollably activating its square to Jupiter - the only major aspect to Jupiter, which is retrograde, and actually rules my empty 1st house?

> *"Do I contradict myself? Very well then, I contradict myself... I am large. I contain multitudes."*
> *WALT WHITMAN*

My chart is contradictory. Each planet, sign and house interferes with the development or satisfaction of another planet, sign or house. Yet, in the words of St. Exupery, I have learned "that each contradiction without solution, each irreparable dispute obliges (me) to grow in order to absorb it." I grow. I grow without limit, extending beyond every barrier. I begin to transcend the oppositions and squares and the other contradictory facets of my chart. The Libra in me, when it confronts and assimilates Aries, discovers the true meaning of harmony and balance and derives unspeakable fulfillment from relationships; Uranus in the 7th, by coming to terms with Venus/Saturn and Moon, stretches her consciousness so wide that it cracks, allowing light to pour in from previously unrevealed dimensions, opening a wide new range of possibilities. I struggle. I curse my chart. But I also bless it, and would not trade one square or opposition for a trine or sextile, even if I could have any trine or sextile I choose.

I grow. In my Sagittarius Rising and 9th house manner, I grow continually, so far, so fast that I frequently must remind myself to stop and digest the understanding I have gained and reflect upon the behaviors I am manifesting, so that each new awareness, each pattern of behavior sinks deeper within me until it reaches the nucleus of my being, and transforms every thought, feeling and action.

I am becoming whole. Slowly, tentatively, with moments of regression, moments of complete disassociation among the disparate parts of myself. But I am becoming whole.

I am ready now to share that wholeness, and all the dissident parts of myself which contribute to my process of integration. Moon in Aries, shaken by the earthquakes of her Uranus square, releases molten fires from the core of the earth, from beneath the waters of the nadir, and flashes these fires so high that they extend far beyond the nadir, inflaming the midheaven and inspiring Neptune to unimaginable heights of poetry.

I am ready to share myself because my progressed

198

Jupiter is turning direct (in the 2nd house by Campanus, 3rd by Placidus) and I am becoming aware of my inner wealth, and believing it worthy of sharing.

I am ready to share myself because Sun and Neptune in Libra are finally beginning to appreciate Moon in Aries, whose self-absorption they had considered a handicap in relationships; they are discovering that Moon's openness and sincerity encourage others to express themselves openly and sincerely, and as a result, to form more fulfilling relationships.

I am ready to share myself because Neptune, who has felt misunderstood by the public because of the vast chasm between her inner and outer selves, is so inflamed by her ideals that she can no longer contain her inspiration, and spills her Piscean waters across the page and into the external domains of my life.

I am ready to share myself because I want others to awaken to the light, to the illumination of the dawn which breaks with a thousand shimmering colors after we have successfully met the droughts of Saturn, the tempests of Uranus, the mists of Neptune and the unfathomable darkness of Pluto. I have experienced the anguish of each of these planets, and still experience that anguish, but know also of the remunerations, the liberations, the revelations and the regenerations that they bring if we refuse to abandon our faith, if we attempt to expand our self-awareness, to uphold our ideals, and like a flower unfolding its petals, to disclose the vast possibilities, the innumerable representations and variations of beauty that arise from the heart of our many selves.

Dynamics of my T-Square

Probably the most dramatic conflict I experience as a result of my t-square is the tension between my determination to remain true to my inner vision, to develop my understanding and operate freely and independently in the world, and an equally insistent craving to be coddled, cuddled and consoled. So easily, I am thrown off balance by relationships which do not sat-

isfy both parts of myself. Those people whom I most respect, who likewise respect my individuality or share
my mission in life, are usually individualists themselves, unwilling to abandon their path long enough to
respond fully to the needs of my Moon; whereas those
watery souls who are so adept at soothing and stilling
the hungers of my Moon and awakening her capacity to be
responsive and nurturing in turn, rarely share the common bonds of understanding and purpose which are to me
a prerequisite for a mutually satisfying and enduring
relationship.

The combination of Neptune in Libra, Uranus in Cancer and Moon in Aries has often been melodramatic. Most
of the relationships which Uranus has discovered (at
least in the past), to the horror of my Venus/Saturn
conjunction, have been with people who are extraordinary, at least by virtue of intellect, but who are also
quite eccentric and frequently unstable. Either the nature of the relationship has been somewhat unusual, due
to the idiosyncrasies of each of us, or my own Neptunian
imagination has dramatized the situation to such an extent that I have felt overcome by my emotional reactions,
and unable to function according to my 9th house standards in most areas of my life.

A second manifestation of my t-square to Uranus is
the emotional intensity, the incessant desire for activity and change, which drives me to push myself so relentlessly to fulfill my ideals and expand my horizons
that I burn myself out, and react passively, oversensi-
tively and sometimes quite irrationally to the interpersonal conflicts which occur in my life.

A third manifestation of my t-square is the gap I
experience between understanding and action (partially
a result of most of my 9th house planets being disassociated, by lack of major aspects, from the rest of my
chart). Sun and Neptune pursue their quest for wisdom
and fulfill their purpose, neglecting to attend to the
needs of Moon; Moon then plunges headlong into new adventures, ignoring Sun's guidance and Neptune's sensitive reactions. Periodically then, Uranus breaks free
from the battle by following some novel and stimulating

course of action apart from other people, or by preoc-
cupying herself with exciting relationships which have
virtually no chance of ever bringing her, Sun, Moon and
Neptune into harmony.

When operating together, the planets in my t-square
are remarkably supportive of each other. Moon lends her
personal approach and her passionate enthusiasm to the
quest of Sun and the mission of Neptune, and helps Uranus to discover stimulating relationships which not only
allow her the freedom to operate according to her own
laws and pursue her own truths, but which are also emotionally nourishing. Sun insures that these relationships are also based upon a common understanding, and
that her own quest for understanding lends substance to
Neptune's aspirations. Pacifying the incessant demands
of Moon, Sun encourages Moon to deliberate before plunging into action, and to consider the delicate feelings
of Neptune. Sun's objectivity, her ability to respond
to each of the planet's needs, as well as her concern
with relationships outside her planetary family, benefit
each member of the t-square configuration.

Neptune also can respond sensitively and compassionately to Moon, as well as to the people important to Sun
in Libra and 7th house Uranus. Her contact with emotional, imaginative and spiritual realms enables Uranus and
Sun to experience the truths which they espouse without
losing themselves in the impersonal domains of intellect.
Neptune infuses all the planets with her sense of meaning, encouraging them to pursue her lofty aims with such
dedication that they are able to transcend their individual needs and cooperate.

Even Uranus is able to contribute to the best interests of the t-square family. Her independent spirit allows Sun to pursue her quest with or without the support
of others, and Moon to actively engage herself in new
projects even when her emotional needs remain unsatis-
fied. The original ideas which Uranus continually generates motivate Moon's activity and stimulate Neptune's
idealism and imagination. Her intuitive and universal
consciousness spurs Moon to draw from her channel at the
nadir, to experience and express that universality of

feeling which lies buried deep within the personal; it encourages Sun to expand her awareness rather than depend upon the insights of others, and Neptune to fulfill her imaginative and spiritual yearnings through literary endeavors which allow her to express her inner truths.

Sun

Sun in Libra in the 9th house is enamored with the panoramic vistas of her inner journeys; she is lured outward to distant places, usually remote and idyllic, where she can be at peace and awaken to the beauties of nature. When Sun was a child, she dialogued with God and affirmed her faith through revelatory experiences which Neptune translated into poetry. As a student majoring in comparative religion, completing her thesis on "the meaning of life," she attempted to synthesize the teachings of innumerable philosophies, religions and psychologies into a coherent whole, and to grasp the universal laws common to diverse pathways. Sun has always been an avid reader, inclined to commune with books which feed her objectivity, and which are also personal, constructive, comprehensive and uplifting.

Sun in Libra in the 9th house identifies with her beliefs and will not compromise her principles. Making choices is difficult for her, because she, like all the other 9th house planets, wants to expand in all directions. Grudgingly, she has allowed Saturn's transit through the 9th house to deprive her of her foreign vacations, if only because Saturn is committed to writing and publishing her books. In addition to writing, publishing and counselling, Sun enjoys teaching, usually one-to-one, or in small groups in which she can relate personally to her students.

In relationships, Sun shies away from confrontations and gravitates toward people with whom she experiences bonds of understanding. Philosophical conflicts are so discomforting to her that she avoids intellectual arguments, as well as people with radically different beliefs who challenge her or arouse her feelings of isolation. Sun is upset by emotional fluctuations which disturb her equilibrium and by relationships in which the give-and-take is out of balance.

Admittedly, Sun wants to be loved by all, but her 9th house principles rarely allow her to play the social games that might win approval. Nonetheless, she frequently thrives on social contact. Bedecked like a princess in various hues of lavender, she loves spending evenings in an exotic coffeehouse or club (usually foreign and always aesthetically pleasing) where she and a special person can exchange ideas, dreams and the intimate matters of their lives. At her best, Sun can be the epitome of charm, sensitively imparting her understanding of others and her concern for their wellbeing, without resorting to the artificial behaviors often characteristic of Libra; Moon in Aries makes sure that her responses are genuine.

Moon

Every planet in my t-square family has at one time or another wanted to blast Moon out of her orbit around the earth and send her hurtling into another solar system.* Probably because her only aspects are squares and oppositions, because she is the Mars/Pluto midpoint, because she is related by the sign of Aries to 12th house Mars, and because the lunar eclipse before her birth endowed her with quite abnormal emotional responses, she is the most unpopular planet in my chart. "I want what I want and I want it *now!*" insists Moon, while the other t-square planets despair at the petulance and reckless abandon with which she disturbs the entire family.

Sun in Libra loses even her tact when compelled to deal with Moon's self-centeredness, and the complete unconsciousness with which Moon overpowers other planets or plunges into unwise activities. Neptune is occasionally embarrassed or reduced to tears when Moon propels all the t-square planets into precarious situations, and she feels victimized when Moon begins so many projects which require her service but do not allow her to dream, meditate or experience the inner silence conducive to inspiration. Uranus can't abide Moon's desire to be protected and comforted, or Moon's tendency to hide away at home

---

THE MIND PARASITES by Colin Wilson is a superb occult novel with a similar theme.

for as long as a week, so preoccupied with her activities that Uranus is unable to break free from the family and bolt out the door in search of exciting diversions.

As a child, Moon hibernated in the nadir of her room, emerging only to indulge in bouts of compulsive eating. Although intensely emotional, she expressed her emotionalism only on the pages of Neptune's poetry or through Neptune's romantic fantasies, and rarely communicated her needs. Now, as she grows up (she's probably about 12), and begins to feel secure with the people in her life, she risks announcing her needs with all the innocence and charm (thanks to Sun in Libra) which she can muster.

"Give me a hug," says Moon, when Neptune is lost in her favorite fantasy novel. "I want some tomatoes," she tells Sun in Libra, who is trying to decide what to do about this chapter's expanding length. Moon then turns to Uranus, who is preparing for a client. "Let me tell you what I did today!"
"You leech! You crybaby! You minx!" shrieks Uranus. "You mollycoddled nincompoop! You whimpering bootlicker! You snivelling bloodsucker! You snot-nosed whippersnapper! You blubbering, puling, mewling dunderhead!!!!!" Uranus zaps Moon in Aries again and again with her electronic tommy gun, amazed at Moon's ability to rise anew from even the most staggering blows.

Usually, Moon seeks refuge in her apartment, journeying only occasionally into the outside world, and dreading, above all, moving day, which on Mercury in Virgo's list of catastrophes and devastations is slightly higher than death and divorce. Rarely angry (12th house Mars sees to that), Moon is nevertheless capable of being quite abrupt with waitresses who serve mayonnaise on her sandwich after she has insisted that they write NO MAYO in capital letters on her check. Usually, she discharges her excess energy by beginning a new project every few days or by provoking Uranus to battle or bolt out of the house in search of excitement.

The other t-square planets often fail to appreciate Moon in Aries' sincerity and candor, and they sometimes underestimate her power. Living as she does precisely on the nadir, at the far midpoint of Mars/Pluto and Sun/ Neptune, she is frequently a channel, capable of drawing from the depths of her psyche and infusing all the planets in the chart with boundless energy and inspiration.

Eclipsed Full Moon

Up and down, high and low, rise and fall, ebb and flow. Sun and Moon ride on a seesaw. Sun is in control for a minute, an hour or even a day, and then Moon takes over, propelling them at such a frenetic speed that the oscillations make them dizzy. After each ride, both are disoriented; they stagger around like lunatics, light-headed and so preoccupied with regaining their sense of reality that they feel disconnected from people around them. Sporadically, Uranus zaps the fulcrum with her electronic tommy gun and the seesaw spins right and left, left and right as well as up and down. Sun and Moon are then disoriented for months, and sometimes years.

Moon's favorite activity is the seesaw. It is the best way she knows to get even with Sun, who longs for balance, but who in a totally uncharacteristic manner annihilated her early in the day. This morning, Moon could have outshone Sun; for once in 28 days she could have experienced the fullness of satisfying all her desires, but Sun eclipsed her. Now Moon, with childish glee, is determined to control the seesaw, to drive it faster and faster, upsetting Sun's equilibrium.

Sometimes, the gyrations of the seesaw thrust Sun and Moon high into the air where for a brief moment they meet and together view the wide vistas stretched below them. Here, in the clarity of the utmost reaches of the atmosphere, Moon illuminates Sun, who later shares the vision and enlightenment they both have experienced. Here, their previous conflicts seem so small, so irrelevant. But Uranus zaps them again, and they go plummeting down.

On earth, Sun and Moon rarely agree about anything, but Sun is so polite that Moon has to assert herself quite forcefully in order to be heard.

"Let's read together and listen to music," suggests Sun. Moon replies, "I want some action." "But I have

*so little energy," sighs Sun. "I'm sure we'd both enjoy
a quiet evening together. Later, Neptune can serve us
wine." "I WANT SOME ACTION!" insists Moon. "You can have
action later," says Sun, "after the wine." "You'll conk
out on me," declares Moon. "I WANT SOME ACTION NOW!!"*

Sun attempts to cooperate; Moon wants her own way.
Sun aims to be objective; Moon can't see beyond her own
needs. Sun evaluates; Moon acts impulsively. Sun desires
peace and balance; Moon, activity and excitement. In addition to all the typical Aries/Libra conflicts, Sun and
Moon are at odds because Sun's eagerness to travel and
explore new realms is threatening to Moon, who clings to
the security of home and to projects which, although often new, are at least familiar and comforting.

The conflict between Sun and Moon is clearly related
to differences between their parents. Their father, of
Romanian Jewish ancestry, is highly emotional, intense,
driving, sociable (p.142). He is 14 years older than
their mother, a Scottish Canadian, and a Virgo/Capricorn,
who is controlled, self-contained and somewhat reclusive.
Sun's major in comparative religion and her subsequent
spiritual development were influenced by her chaotic religious upbringing. First, she attended Catholic mass with
a governess, then Baptist Sunday school with a friend,
then temple (at the insistence of father), then Presbyter-
ian church (at the insistence of mother), and then, after
singing "Jesus loves me" one day in the living room,
temple again for five more years. Moon, as a result, has
felt insecure in both Christian and Jewish settings, and
is convinced that she doesn't really belong anywhere except at home on the nadir; there, she turns inward and
develops her own personal religion, somewhat inspired by
the spiritual quest of Sun.

Sun and Moon were born only hours after full Moon. At
their best, they experience "a life spent in the wake of
a vision."* The heights above the seesaw awaken a clarity
of consciousness in which all the battles of the t-square
family and the vistas of the world in which they live are
as vivid and distinct as trees after rain.

Busteed, Tiffany and Wergin, PHASES OF THE MOON

When they were children, Sun's friend Neptune intro-
duced them to the revelations of nature and of poetry.
In late adolescence, bombarded by a stationary Uranus,
the three of them experienced trances and perceived diagrams of the universe which they were unable to translate
into any intelligible language. How they struggled then,
in isolation, to maintain their contact with reality!
Now, as adults, they seek to understand their illumina-
tions, and to impart their far-flung vision in words that
are profound and poetic and personal.

At this moment, at the peak of their progressed full
Moon, as they write this chapter, they gaze at each other
in awe and wonder. All is luminous. All is boundless. All
they are, all they see, is infused with meaning.

Neptune

With Sun in Libra, her female companion, Neptune in
Libra in the 10th house shares the honor of being the
most elevated planet in my chart. Neptune is a poet. She
is also a mystic. Shy and elusive, she weaves a tapestry
of spells about the midheaven. Enshrouded by mist, when
none can see her, she sings her melodies and pirouettes
across the firmaments. Neptune is at home in the heights;
she converses with the angels, and translates their celestial music into her own ethereal harmonies.

When Neptune was a child living with a Piscean family in the 3rd house, North Node inspired her to write
reams of poetry. Rarely would she sleep, because each
poem invoked a trance that remained unbroken until dawn.
Starry-eyed and struck often to tears by her visions and
revelations, Neptune invoked her Muse to write lyrics to
her romantic and mystical yearnings, or to spill upon
the page the agonies of having no companions who understood the mysteries of her soul. During early adolescence,
when Jupiter transited her 3rd house and the progressed
Sun approached conjunction, Neptune wrote at least one
poem a night. In *"Stardust,"* she attempted to come to
terms with Moon in Aries. In *"Beauty of the Dawn,"* she
revealed her growing friendship with Sun.

If only Neptune hadn't been born near the midheaven!
Sensitive to daylight, she never seems able to avoid the

POEMS BY NEPTUNE

poems by Tracy Marks, from her junior high school
collection of poetry, *And Still the Birds Sing*

STARDUST (1963)

Gazing in awe at the glimmering stars,
Alone in an enchanted land,
I flung out my arms to the night's subtle magic,
And some stardust fell in my hand.

I was so thrilled and full of wonder.
A little stardust could bring me much wealth.
I bought joy and pleasure, love and laughter -
Contentments, but all for myself.

Last night I stood under that silvery sky
And the countless stars still shone.
But when I held out my hand to catch more stardust,
I found that it was gone.

BEAUTY OF THE DAWN (1963)

When the dawn awakens
From her lengthy sleep,
Her hazy splendor casts a spell
Till beauty is waist deep.

When the sun turns on its light
At the start of a new day,
A miracle is taking place.
Beauty has her say.

From the early skies of morning,
Silvery blue, pink and gold,
We will find the source of beauty
In our hearts to ever hold.

With colors, colors of the rainbow,
Even more, their splendor hurled
Across the sky, we'll paint the beauty.
We'll share our canvas with the world.

glaring rays of noon. Magazines sought her out, and newspapers; literary clubs presented awards and requested her to read in vast auditoriums teeming with people. Neptune, who preferred silence to applause, was too delicate for crowds; she absorbed their suffering, their fears, their joys, and trembled, close to tears. The energy of Moon and Uranus was all that she could handle. Her teachers also praised their ideal student, whose inspiration extended to even the most mundane of subjects, but such praise only meant that Neptune had to grapple with being misunderstood by her classmates.

(Progressed Uranus turning stationary then provoked such a crisis that Neptune abandoned her poetry to serve her planetary family. As transiting Neptune entered the 12th house, the floodwaters of creativity seeped underground, only to emerge upon rare occasions, and the gentle currents of spirituality and compassion reawakened Neptune's idealism. Neptune then rose from the 3rd house, and established herself more fully in the 10th.)

With a clarity of vision which astounds even Uranus, Neptune has always conceived of her mission in life; the form has changed, but the message never alters. When she was six and first invoked her Muse, she knew she was destined to be a writer. At eight, she determined that her mission was to help other people tap their own sources of inspiration. Illumined by the empyreal realms in which she resides, Neptune remains true to her vision, although she neglects the material needs of the other planets, and is lost in a fog of confusion in regard to realities of the external world. Neptune has a gift, and she has dedicated her life to giving it. There is a tinge of the martyr about her, because she asks for so little in return, but she is absorbing from Moon in Aries the ability to go after what she wants, and Neptune wants the time and space and silence and solitude to continue singing.

Uranus

Zap. Whiz. Smash. Bam. Thud. Uranus in Cancer in the 7th house is particularly cantankerous today. He hurls the pages of this chapter around the room, refusing to cooperate. "You ain't gonna trap me between no covers of a book!" he bellows. He glares at the plan of the book and discovers the limited space allotted to him. "Man, you only left me a few pages!" he protests. "I got to have my freedom! You ain't gonna set no limits on me!"

He? Yes, Uranus is a he. He keeps changing sex; he now insists that the Uranus appearing on earlier pages is his sister, Uranus Retrograde, who by progression is gaining influence in the t-square family. "Don't you dare call me female!" threatens Uranus. "I'm a man." He struts around the room, puffing up his chest in a display of bravado. "I'm tough. I'm strong. I'm free. I'm my own person!!... Females," he guffaws. "Females are SOPPY!" To emphasize the point, he grabs his electronic tommy gun and shoots six bullseyes into the center of the light socket. The sparks fly in all directions.

Living as he does with Sun, Moon and Neptune, Uranus certainly has a right to his opinion. Sun in Libra cries when people don't smile at her, Neptune weeps poetry on the page when people do, and Moon in Aries wails whenever she doesn't get her way. "Mush!" snorts Uranus. "Them other planets. Sodden soggy soppy watery mush!!"

"Uranus," I tell him, appealing to his Cancerian attraction to exotic foods (which Moon, of course is unable to digest), "Uranus, suppose we're preparing a gourmet dish, and we add three delicacies. Let's call them Sun, Moon and Neptune. Now, let's say we subject them to an electric beater and leave it whirring for days and days. What happens to our three delicacies?"

"MUSH!" grins Uranus, sparkling like the light socket. His eyes gleam. He whizzes around the room in search of a new target.

"Uranus," I ask him. "Who do you think is that electric beater? Who do you think is responsible for the mush?"

Uranus zaps me. His eyes dart from left to right as he tries to break out of the corner in which I've placed him. He shifts his feet. He swaggers. "Man," he tells me. "I'm just trying to build their character....Those three, they ain't got no resistances. Man, you got to have resistances to make it in this world, this hellhole," he sputters. "You can't let nothing get to you, man. You trust

*no one. You don't get close to no one. All you got is
yourself, and if you don't protect that, man, you're
gonna be mush like them!"*

*"I've been zapped," Uranus continues. "I don't let
nobody zap me no more. You get zapped enough, man, and
you learn to zap back them bullets....Neptune, Moon,
Sun," he grimaces. "They got a lot to learn from me."*

*"Uranus," I gape at him, astonished at the character
who stepped out of my 7th house, whom I would never have
believed existed inside me, but who bears an uncomfortable resemblance to certain key men in my past. "Uranus,"
I say. "Maybe you're going about it the wrong way. Maybe
what you need, maybe what they need, is a little love."*

*"LOVE?" sputters Uranus, and squints at me, trying
to determine what trick I'm playing. "LOVE?" he scoffs.
"PHOOEY! Love is SOPPY! They don't need no love. I don't
need no love. Just give me my freedom, man, and I can
make bells ring, and they ain't the bells of no church
wedding!" But his voice is shaky, irregular. It rises
too high and drops too low. Uranus is disconcerted.
"Love," he blurts out. "What's it all about, anyway?"*

Uranus is an acrobat. He straddles that fine, fine
line between genius and madness. Despite the mush he'd
become if he slipped from the tightrope, he performs
somersaults and cartwheels on the wire, astounding Sun
and Neptune in Libra with his various contortions at
high altitudes. If they, attempting to maintain their
balance, falteringly step into his path, he simply
shoves them into the pit below, and continues with his
calisthenics. Uranus doesn't believe he needs anyone,
which means, of course, that he is often left alone to
cope with the convolutions of his own psyche.

When Uranus was a child, he was convinced that he
was an alien from a distant galaxy. For years, he was
fearful of bleeding (12th house Mars), lest doctors examine him and discover his outlandish chemistry. His
parents were aliens themselves, but from what Uranus regarded to be an antagonistic universe, and even his own
planetary family did not know how to cope with the ren-
egade in their midst. Later, Uranus was to confirm his

211

T-SQUARE TO URANUS

Alienation

childhood poems by Tracy Marks, from her junior high
school poetry collection, *And Still the Birds Sing*

THE CHOICE (1963)

Oh, I can be social
   And make life a game,
Let my inner self
   Rot away.

Or I can be me,
   Alone, but free,
And fully experience
   Each day.

Which is the best?
   I have my choice,
To choose one or the other -
   Either.

But it really is hard
   To be what I am,
Both in a way, yet
   Neither.

INNOCENCE (1964)

They called me names,
And I laughed in their faces.
I said they were wrong,
But I didn't belong,
So they laughed in mine.

I was a freak, a square, a reject,
They said, different from everyone else.
But how could I be
Unlike the real me,
Unlike what I always was?

Amidst them each day, but not a part,
I was never free from their stares
Till I turned to go home,
By myself, all alone
With my tears.

TETRAMETER SONNET (1965)

Don't pity me; I live my life
   And try my best in all I do.
If I find loneliness or strife,
   I'll learn from it more than from you.
Don't scoff at me, for I am true
   To my beliefs, whether right or wrong.
We're not the same. Can't you perceive
   That I don't care whether I BELONG?
I know my character will improve,
   But how and when are my concern.
If you think you're helping me, then you've
   Got quite a lot about me to learn.
Why ask me to conform? I stress,
I am myself - no more, no less.

belief by discovering on his family's heliocentric chart a t-square to earth, a discovery that sent Moon into convulsions of laughter.

Gradually, because he was incapable of conforming, Uranus began to take pride in his uniqueness. Determined to exist apart from the crowd, he decided to be as different as possible. Uranus was adept at doing the opposite of what he was supposed to do. Since his father was preoccupied with influencing his children's lives (p.142 locomotive to 5th house Uranus, t-squares to 9th house Moon in Taurus and 8th house Mars in Aries), Uranus had many opportunities for rebellion. After awhile, he refused to do so many things that no options remained, and the realms in which he lived grew so narrow that he, who demanded freedom, could barely move. Progressed Uranus then was stationary.

The crisis which Uranus experienced disrupted the entire t-square family for several years. Neptune, unable to write poetry, became victim to hallucinations; Moon, feeling undernourished, ate ten meals a day; Sun in Libra, unable to form meaningful outside relationships, cooperated with the other 9th house planets, and focused, somewhat obsessively, upon her religious studies, attempting to develop the faith and understanding necessary to survive the crisis. Uranus, who refused to depend upon others, was rescued then, just in time, by his sister — Uranus Retrograde.

Uranus Retrograde came streaking into the world fresh from an encounter group, with a scarf of astrological symbols fluttering behind her. She had invented her own system for understanding the complexities of the psyche and communicated it to Uranus when he was a child (Mercury in Virgo transcribed it in a notebook), so he could relate to the archetypes she now taught him. Uranus Retrograde guided Uranus up the path of humanistic psychology and down the path of astrology and eventually brought him back to where he stood and said, *"Take all I've taught you, and let it be a guide. But now, blaze your own path. Blaze a path that leads to people and not apart from them. Discover the universal realms, the truths that lie in you. You are your own liberation."*

Uranus Retrograde zapped Uranus with *her* electronic
tommy gun and Uranus was stunned by the light that broke
around him. It didn't put him to sleep at all, as his
own electronic tommy gun sometimes put Sun, Moon and
Neptune to sleep. Instead, it awakened him.

Uranus looked within and looked without. He experienced the bonds that linked him to humanity, the interdependence that makes independence actually possible. He
learned and obeyed the laws of his own being, no longer
needing to rebel in order to maintain his identity. A
streak of the rebel remained, nonetheless, for Uranus
now rebelled against the anguish of his alienated childhood and the claustrophobia of the stationary period
during which he could barely breathe. Uranus rebelled
by announcing what an aware, evolved, sensitive and capable being he would become, despite all the obstacles
on his self-chosen path.

*"I ain't gonna be a tragic figure no more!" protests
Uranus, gazing up at Neptune who is writing poems to
Heathcliffe from her wuthering heights.*

*"I ain't gonna stand outside the world and swear
'cause I don't belong!" he declares to Moon, who has
retreated once again to her nadir.*

*He turns to Sun. "I ain't gonna zap at people no
more with no E-LEC-tronic tommy gun and make 'em dizzy
or put 'em to sleep. No, that ain't the way, man," he
shakes his head. "I'm gonna zap 'em with LIGHT!"*

*"I'm tough. I'm strong. I'm free. I'm my own per-
son!" asserts Uranus. "And I'm even gonna swim in that
there mush with Sun, Moon and Neptune 'cause I know now
that it takes one hell of a lot more strength and guts
to swim in that mush with them and walk out of it whole
than it does to do somersaults on a tightrope while
Sun, Moon and Neptune drown!"*

*"I'm gonna help 'em," he tells me. "I'm gonna help
'em learn to swim 'cause they're my family and friends,
and man, you got to have friends, 'cause without them,
man, then what's it all about...anyway?"*

214

URANUS, THE LIBERATOR

by Tracy Marks

Uranus,
you shatter and smash
my consciousness.
You fling me mercilessly
from universe to universe.

I dance on electric particles.
My veins throb
with your alternating current.
You magnetize me.

I repel
the electrostatic charge
of your embrace
and turn away from you,
but my other pole
attracts you back again.

Uranus,
I quiver at your touch.
You streak through me
with the frenzy of lightning.

Your agita   tions, instiga
*   tions, pulsa   tions,*
stimula   tions, muta
*   tions, devia   tions,*
*   tions, fluctua   tions,*
aliena   tions, alterna
detona   tions, experimenta
*   tions, dramatiza   tions,*
*   tions, libera   tions,*
innova   tions, transforma

leave me quaking
leave me   breaking
leave me   waking, Uranus.

Uranus. Uranus. You send waves of electricity racing down my spine. How you change! How you transform me!

Sometimes, you fling me around so mercilessly that the electrons of my psyche crash like dodgem cars and I am seared by the sparks. A Daedalus, an Icarus, you reach too high. You open the gateways of my 9th house. You conduct the currents of your quintiles and electrify my consciousness. You steal the Sun's chariot and soar across the sky; you glide on the wings of Neptune. Electricity was not meant to fly, Uranus. There's fire in those heights. We scorch; we burn. Our wings melt; our chariot veers off course and plunges toward the mush below, the wild Cancerian waters. Why, Uranus? Why?

"I'm gonna take ev'ry 'xperience far as it goes," declares Uranus. "Nobody ever gonna say I ain't lived!"

You live. You live. A master mind, a whiz, at times you flash with genius. But your flashes wreak havoc in my life, Uranus. You disrupt me. You disrupt my 7th house, my 2nd house. You singe the structure of my day. Clients, students, friends - you push them away to shoot your sparks of electricity through me. I become an electromagnet like you, Uranus. I attract; I repel. I repel; I attract. Those drawn to me respond to your magnetism; I did not recognize that they share the same magnetism. You attract dramatic, disruptive people into my life, Uranus. And then you push them all away.

Perhaps I have not fully owned you. Perhaps I have not called you by my name. I need no disruptive people in my life, Uranus. My Moon cries for more; Venus/Saturn knocks at the door of my psyche and says:

"Enough. Enough. The time has come to learn about setting limits. I bring liberation too."

Relationships

Uranus really doesn't know what to make of Venus/Saturn - conservative, security-oriented Venus/Saturn, who shuns one night stands, married men and open relationships, who demands men she can respect, men who are dedicating their lives to a higher purpose, who are loyal, committed and above all, reliable (usually double Capricorns). Unwilling to tolerate such tedium, Uranus waits until Venus/Saturn is buried in her work, flashes her electromagnetic rays and brings home the most outlandish, the most unconventional, the most bizarre Capricornian or Saturnian men ever to visit the planet earth - devils lurking beneath a staid and stable demeanor! And Venus/ Saturn falls for them! Poor Venus/Saturn! She never knows what's happening until it's too late; then she retreats once again into her day and night vigil of work in order to extinguish the pangs of loss. Most of the time, except when cooperating on a book, Venus/Saturn and Uranus ignore each other, linked as they are by only a quintile. But when that quintile is awakened, for however long, no planetary combination or aspect can equal the delights of that magic!

The story of my intimate relationships during my twenties,* under a stationary retrograde Uranus, could be entitled, "The Saga of the Double Capricorns," or "Close Encounters with the 10th Sign." I should be wary when climbing mountains, I tell myself, for instead of mountain goats I discover aliens residing on those peaks - Uranian souls trapped in Capricornian bodies. How do I find them all?, I wonder - the double Capricorns or men with Sun, Moon or Ascendant in Capricorn and a prominent Saturn or 10th house? Are all Capricornian men as bizarre as the ones I have known?

You have flashed such blinding light, Uranus Retrograde. How solid, how stable they seemed! How they concealed their idiosyncrasies! With planets trining Moon and the tender, delicate touch of Pisces trining Uranus, they've inspired Neptune to song. But why the Capricorn, Uranus? (And *why* the *Uranus*, Capricorn?)

Once progressed Uranus was clearly retrograde, my relationship patterns changed significantly. My life during my thirties includes a predominance of Cancer/Pisces men and women - the opposite polarity of Capricorn/Virgo. One factor influencing this change is a therapeutic experience during which I came to terms more fully with my Moon, and my intercepted 7th house Cancer energies. As progressed planets in Scorpio trine my Uranus, my focus has also shifted from 7th house to 11th house relationships.

As I watch the splinters of light emerge and disappear as clouds conceal the sun, I begin to understand the lesson of waiting. The passing of clouds is beyond my control; I can only respond. Like the clouds, my many selves pass over me, changing interminably - writer, star, fairy princess, wallflower, loner, sensual woman, hungry child, creative thinker, loyal friend, woman in love. As each cloud is an integral part of the sky, each of my selves is an integral part of me. Each one passes over me and makes room for another as long as I don't cling to it because I value it much more than another part, or fight it because I reject the qualities it embodies.

Who then am I? I am the one who watches the passing of clouds.

I did not belong to the group on Pinckney avenue. For a year I lived with them, but left the dinner table early and read in my room when they had parties downstairs. What is wrong with me?, I asked myself, cringing. Why must I hold myself apart? Why can't I enjoy their company? Why am I always the black sheep, the albatross, the butterfly with one wing?

Now, three years later, I look back in disbelief at the pain of that year in which I felt I was wrong for not adapting, when I indeed I WAS wrong, but in choosing the wrong group. I stumbled upon new friends the day I decided to flaunt the bright yellow and green of my healthy wing rather than shake my stub of a broken wing at nearby predators. And they welcomed me, the other one-winged butterflies.

I realized then that I could not belong everywhere, and still belong to myself.

I feared you would not accept my secret self, that wild rough rampant creature within me which bursts free of every bond and delights in tumult and frenzy. I too judged myself and believed I should submit to restraints not of my choosing. And yet the roaring and thrashing would overcome me; never would I willingly be tamed.

I feared that when you saw, you would condemn me, believing me unworthy, hiding from yourself your envy. Your wildness was not equal to my own.

And when my fear came true, I defended that tempestuous unicorn in me, whose maddened boltings from her stall and raucous snorts had always appalled me. And I realized then, exposing her, protecting her, how much I loved her, and that within her lived my passion and my power, and those creative surgings which require the temperament to kick down stalls, break the harness of old realities and roam freely, trespassing into forbidden lands.

We entangled our dreams together, and in doing so entwined our souls. Our dream was an extension of us; it took root and grew like a sunflower, watered by devotion to a mission which transcended ourselves. How I sought that common vision; how I fed off that liquid magic, expecting the rain to replenish the waters of early spring, unprepared for the ravages of a sudden storm.

And the death of that DREAM, rooted deep within the recesses of my being, the violent rending of a flower before summer, was a greater loss than losing you. For when the dream shattered, I shattered too.

I won't twist another in my dream again. And you who join me now, nurture your own dream while I nurture mine. And when our dreams meet, let us be like two flowers sharing the same sun, the same wind, the same rain, nodding and brushing our petals against each other, rejoicing in our togetherness, affirming our uniqueness, retaining our separateness.

Before I became addicted to mountain goats, or at
least to Uranians masquerading as mountain goats, my Ura-
nus/Moon square dominated my chart. Moon, after all, was
raised by a succession of governesses. One would leave
suddenly, and the next would appear, only to disappear
unexpectedly in a few month's time. Mother was always
ill, hospitalized, recovering from surgery, lingering
on the verge of death. Her 9 Cancer Pluto conjuncts Uranus and squares Moon, who was so flooded with Neptune's
tears that expressing any emotion swept her away on a
tidal wave. It was easier not to make contact at all.

Moon never understood how, after that, she became
close to women. There were years of broken friendships,
but after Uranus Retrograde zapped her with light, Moon
drew water signs to her, female Pisces and Scorpios
trining Uranus, with planets or angles conjuncting Moon.
But first Moon in Aries had to begin all over - to leave
one family, to discover her planetary family, new friends,
a new home, and even a new name. Moon has few conflicts
with women now; Uranus prefers to create havoc with men.

The most important of them all was a double Capri-
corn/Virgo, with Sun and Ascendant opposing Uranus, and
his Moon at the end of his own t-square, conjuncting my
Venus/Saturn. With him, Moon felt bathed in the nourishing waters of love, and began to learn how, in turn, to
become nourishing. She and Uranus, after conjuncting
near the descendant of a solar return, cooperated for
three years. In the end, it wasn't Uranus that zapped
Moon, but two eclipses, triggering both our t-squares.

*"What's it all about, anyway?" Sun asks Uranus. "The
double Capricorns? The empty Capricorn in our 1st house?
We want to understand the relationships you bring."*

*"Hey, don't rush me, man!" replies Uranus. "We got
one more CA-TA-stro-phee we gotta deal with. You ain't
gonna avoid this one." He points his electronic tommy
gun right between Sun's eyes, and then hurls it on the
ground. "Light ain't free anymore," declares Uranus.
"'Lectricity ain't cheap. If we're gonna be zapped
with light from now on, man....we gotta pay for it!"*

Uranus Square Moon

"It's the Last Judgment!" Moon in Aries screams, delirious with fever. She screams again. "It's the end of our world!"

Fires. Floods. Quakes. Lightning. Squalls. Comets are streaking through the solar system, spewing flames across the sky, veering toward Moon. She writhes; she thrashes. Neptune from her heights weeps radiation clouds; earth teeters on its axis. Sun in Libra, scales now out balance, loses consciousness.

"Uranus!" I shriek. "Stop! Stop killing our family!"

"It ain't me," Uranus mutters. "It ain't me at all. This time, it's Uranus Retrograde."

We have an illness, one resistant to cure. Neptune hesitates to share such delicate matters, but it is such an obvious manifestation of our t-square that she must be overruled. Frequently, unexpectedly, spasms rack our body - contractions, we've been told, up to ten times stronger than those of labor, and lasting up to ten times as long. Never do we know how many projects, classes, clients must be cancelled, how many hours will be needed when we're well again to make up for lost time. It all began after Uranus turned retrograde.

We try all the cures, to no avail, and retreat into Neptune opposition Moon passivity. How often we view with horror instead of awe the electricity racing through our body, tearing it apart. How often we must renew our will to live.

This is no becoming whole. This is no enlightenment. This is no price to pay for illumination.

The planets moan like characters out of Job after each cataclysm, and beseech Uranus Retrograde:

"You sure are some hell of a lightbearer!" bellows Uranus, his eyes flashing sparks of fury. "We ain't gonna put up with your shenanigans!" Uranus Retrograde doesn't answer.

"You've betrayed us, Uranus Retrograde," sobs Neptune. Uranus Retrograde doesn't answer.

"I've been good! I've been good!" wails Moon in Aries.

"I haven't been bad! Go away, oh go away, Uranus Retrograde!" Uranus Retrograde doesn't answer.

"Tell us why. We want to understand," beseeches Sun from her 9th house. Uranus Retrograde doesn't answer.

Uranus zaps at the air where Uranus Retrograde once stood and zapped him with light. His eyes spark with anger. "She ain't gonna help us," declares Uranus. "We gotta figger things out ourselves." Uranus begins to figger. He figgers so hard, he figgers so long, his brain short circuits and flames rage around the t-square family. Uranus looks about him. He sees his fires smoldering above the earth, the devastations of his electricity.

"Maybe it's 'cause I ain't grounded," he says. "Maybe it's 'cause there ain't no Capricorn in our 1st house."

The Empty Space

Grounded? What's it all about anyway, Uranus? I'm only beginning to learn. I know when you speak I sprawl upon the floor to write; no other planets demand such posture. Any contact with you sends me plummeting toward earth.

Grounded? Perhaps that is, after all, the key to the empty space of my t-square - Capricorn in the 1st house. For years, surrounded by Capricorn Suns and Ascendants, I have attempted to understand it. The qualities of Capricorn are qualities I've lacked and have struggled to develop - stability, practicality, emotional control, self-protectiveness (a filtering system which keeps one from being overwhelmed with one's own and other people's feelings), ambition (not in regard to fulfilling an ideal, but in regard to establishing oneself in society), and the ability to determine priorities, to focus upon one task and follow it through to completion, as well as a sense of limits. Virgo has enabled me to work diligently and efficiently, to be responsible, committed and loyal, but Virgo is not Capricorn, and the 9th house is not as solid and reality-based as the 1st.

I have, over time, begun to understand several of the meanings of my empty space, apart from the issues related to grounding. Years of feeling powerless and out of control of my life have motivated me to discover how I and other people can begin to master planetary energies, rather than remain helpless victims, unwilling to take responsibility for our actions. Years of striving to understand myself have led me, upon occasion, to experience the full power of "I know who I am," apart from intellectual clarifications which are no substitute at all for the core experience.

Never having learned to play a role or pay attention to how I project myself, I always believed, and still believe, in being "real" and sincere, but sincerity never helped me teach high school or adapt to many social situations. Always, too, I rebelled against my Miami background by refusing to be concerned with externals, packaging of any kind, considering people who cultivated their appearance to be superficial. I know better now. As Jupiter, my ascendant ruler, turned stationary and I began to value and nourish my Moon, I shed my 30 excess pounds; as Jupiter turns direct, I cut my waist length hair, trade granny glasses for contact lenses, throw out my jeans and slowly expand my lavender wardrobe. I discover the extent to which my appearance influences my internal state, enabling me not only to remain in contact with myself and enjoy my physical presence, but also at times to manifest the beauty I have been attempting to develop inwardly all my life.

I understand too the empty degree of my t-square - "an albatross feeding from the hand of a sailor....the overcoming of fear and its rewards...trust."(My favorite poem as a child, Baudelaire's *"Albatross,"* describes the poet as an albatross - awkward on land, sublime in the air.) I have known fear, fear so vast that when Pluto conjuncted my Sun and I expressed it, the windows shattered, so powerful was my voice. I have not known trust. Venus/Saturn doesn't trust; Uranus doesn't trust. They never had reason to trust; they realized at an early age that nothing outside oneself is solid or stable or lasting or can provide a reliable support. Perhaps as I own my Uranus and develop Capricorn, I can transcend them both and begin to trust, but I am not convinced that the realization I had a child is invalid.

These lessons are not all the lessons of my empty space; there remains still the lesson of grounding. I study electricity and learn that grounding a wire allows for the safe discharge of excess energy and prevents a sudden build-up of charge from burning out a part of the system or causing a fire. I study bioenergetics, and discover that I have all the characteristics of an ungrounded person – no feeling in my feet (Pisces), high excitation, a flushed face, raised shoulders, a fearful expression often concealing anger. Ungrounded people are easily overwhelmed by high levels of energy; ungrounded people give away their power; ungrounded people hear the continual chatter of their planetary voices and rarely know internal silence. I decide to become grounded.

I begin dance classes; I learn bioenergetic exercises to facilitate grounding. But I resist; I resist with intensity, avoiding the slightest exertion. I curse my Libra Sun, my 12th house Mars; their sextile reinforces their distaste for exercises, particularly painful exercises enabling me to become grounded. I recall the humiliation of failing every physical fitness test, the report cards bearing D's in gym. Is this where it all began?

To battle a resistance is to bash my head against a wall; I must stand back and survey the wall, speak with it, discover its nature, learn how to walk around it or leap over it. I look deeper. Fear grows within me. If I were grounded, would I lose the inspiration, the illumination? Would Neptune fall from her heights? I look deeper still. Fear overwhelms me – fear of my own power. I have shattered windows with my voice, have shaken for days after Chopin came through me, have experienced when outer planets transited my Midheaven (Mars/Pluto) frightening manifestations of power unleashed around and within me. I have every reason to fear the power that resides within my body, but because I will not choose to experience it and own it, that power wreaks havoc upon me, weakening me month after month, year after year.

I know that if I am not to be destroyed by it, I must expand my capacity to handle it. I must become grounded. But the planets in my chart rebel at the exercises; none will exert themselves. This must not be my way. Only the Self that begins to emerge in me, that transcends and *includes* all my planetary selves can reveal my path toward grounding. All my planets must agree to be grounded, must commit themselves to this task, before the Self will reveal how such grounding will take place.

I begin to strengthen my will. I undergo nutritional tests and discover deficiencies related to Capricorn and Pisces - Pisces, my North Node, weakened by its oppositions, ruler of the feet. Energy must flow through my feet if I am to be grounded.

With Progressed Moon in Taurus, I am pulled down toward the core of the earth. Moon in Aries has tried to ground me in fire, and fire burns the earth; yet I've had to journey through fire to reach the nadir of my being. Mars/Pluto midpoint, aren't you, Moon? What secrets do you guard at the nadir? Does earth lie beneath your fire? Will accepting you, expressing you, lead me to grounding?

I begin to embrace the earth. "This is the earth, the kingdom I've been looking for," I quote some half-forgotten monument. For what value are the heights unless my feet are planted firmly on the ground?

But inside me, Neptune sobs. "Neptune," I tell her gently, "Perhaps now Moon will have an inner home and not need to cling to her outer home, and Sun in Libra will regain her balance and Uranus will spark his quintile to Saturn and awaken us all with grounded electricity."
Neptune sobs still. Her tears shed torrents of rain; the earth becomes grey and drab without her music. "Will I continue singing?" she asks me, trembling.
"Yes," I tell her, and "yes" again, with more assurance and with infinite tenderness, for Neptune is my chosen one, the dearest of all my planetary selves. "You will sing with more richness, more fullness, more resonance now, and the earth as well as the heights will resound with your song."

Uranus/Saturn

Saturn. Uranus. You are my teachers; together I must incorporate you into my life. I calculate my navamsa chart, the chart which reveals the path of the soul's evolution, and discover Uranus at 24 Virgo 0 minutes, the position of my natal Saturn. I ask the Astro-Dice, "What am I to learn from my t-square to Uranus?" and roll Saturn in Capricorn in the 7th house. "How can I best express it?" Saturn in Capricorn in the 5th house. "How do I develop my empty space?" Saturn in Virgo in the 1st house. "Is my task now that of grounding?" North Node in Taurus in the 1st house. "How can I integrate all my planetary selves?" Uranus in Capricorn in the 7th house.

I have experienced how negative Saturn leads to negative Uranus; early deprivations led me to rebel and become alienated from other people. I have experienced how negative Uranus leads to negative Saturn; such rebellion limited my options until none remained and I was left alone, despondent, locked within the prison of my psyche. I experience now how positive Uranus leads to positive Saturn and how positive Saturn leads to positive Uranus, and I dialogue with Saturn and Uranus, asking them what lessons they have to teach me.

Saturn is tall, elderly. He stands erect or sits upright in a chair - an electric chair if Uranus is nearby, but Saturn is never harmed by the electricity. Sturdy, stable, he keeps his feet anchored firmly on the ground, like a veritable rock of solidity. When he speaks, his voice is low, sonorous, often solemn.

"You are learning the lesson of grounding," Saturn informs me. "Lesson two is the lesson of security -"

"There ain't none!" interrupts Uranus, sparking Saturn's chair up to its highest voltage. "It's all change, man, it's all process. You gotta let go, man, 'cause if you trust anything at all, trust that where you are today, man, you won't be tomorrow. Not if I'm around."

"Correct," continues Saturn, "except for one important matter. If you experience in the bedrock of your being your ultimate insecurity, if your aim is your own development and you trust that each change whether great or small will strengthen your character, then you are instantly secure."

"Right on, Saturn!" applauds Uranus. "And look what I do, man! Each time I spark my 'lectricity, each time I scatter your 'lectrons across the room, you gotta pull yourself together, you gotta build your char'cter. Ain't it great, man?" Uranus glows with light. "Soon as I 'rive on the scene, man, you gotta learn Saturn."

I look at them both, somewhat bedazzled. "So that's what all those Uranian Capricorns are about," I say. Because I can't rely on them, I develop security within myself. I learn the lessons of Saturn. *("And look how in-DEE-pendent you become too, man," adds Uranus.)*

"Lesson three," expounds Saturn, "is the lesson of the law-("Call it freedom, man!" interrupts Uranus)-the lesson of freedom. There are laws within you that transcend your many selves, that link you to the universal Self. If you are true to those laws, you are instantly free."

"But you can't play no tricks on yourself!" interrupts Uranus. "Man, you can't do no acrobatics with your planetary fam'ly and PREE-tend that one of them is the voice of all. No, that ain't the way, man!"

"Go beyond each planet," advises Saturn. "In the silence beneath the voices is the voice of the Self, the voice that encompasses all of your selves. It is the law in you and you will know it because all of your planets will agree to it, and because it is not at odds with the laws around you."

"It's the truth, man," announces Uranus. "It's your own pers'nal truth and it's the u-NEE-versal truth and there ain't no greater freedom, man, than what you feel when you listen to it and live by it and have the guts to walk along its path."

"To live in this world," expostulates Saturn. "You conform. But you conform to that which accords with your inner law."

"You can do it!" adds Uranus. "Man, you can do it. You can do it and be true to who you are."

"I am learning that lesson," I tell them. "But this year, I questioned the laws of my being. I followed those laws, but they led me to work day and night without food, without sleep, without contact with friends. And even then I could not survive in this world. I wondered if I were listening to the voice of one or two of my planets and not the voice beyond them all. But I know," I affirm, "I know and all my planets know that it is the Self that

227

directs me, and that the Self directs me to write."

"This summer," I explain to Saturn. "Mercury made a list of books she longed to write, ideas she wished to express, and despaired because many were not practical. Too few people would read them; too few are pursuing similar truths. The Self then directed us to the library. We did market research; we learned what people buy. We discovered books which speak the truth that appeal to many people. They speak to all of humanity, to many selves, and not only to Uranus, not only in a jargon that few can understand. Neptune has a dream," I reveal to Saturn. "At night, she dreams of writing another *Little Prince*."

"You are learning lesson four," proclaims Saturn, "the lesson of society. For where your laws intersect society's laws, there is your liberation." Saturn shows me a diagram that Mercury and Venus have drawn, and informs me, "As I speak to you now, it is the time of my Return. I face transiting Saturn. Together, we say to you that when you face society, where you meet society, there is a circle to celebrate your meeting. And that is the circle of your liberation. For two Saturns facing each other and a circle enjoining them yield -"

"Man!" howls Uranus, and grabs the diagram from Saturn's hands, spinning Saturn's electric chair up to the ceiling and then back down to the ground. "That's me! That's Uranus!"

"Two Saturns yield one Uranus," continues Saturn. "The lessons of Saturn are the lessons of liberation."

"I feel liberated now," I tell Saturn. "Aloneness, focus, a clear sense of priorities, months of accomplishment. I have given up so much, and yet I gain so much more."

"That's lesson five. Slow down!" rebukes Saturn. "Before we cover lesson five, you must relearn lesson one." Saturn beckons to Mercury and Venus in Virgo, who draw the chart of our planetary family. "Here is Neptune," he points to the 10th house. "And here is transiting Neptune asleep in the 12th. She is beginning to wake, to cross the

ascendant and approach the empty space. Because of the years she has been sleeping, dreaming her music, the music she will sing could sweep you away," Saturn slams his feet on the earth, "unless you are grounded."

"You must be of the earth," Saturn continues, "to write for the earth. You must be of the earth, or Neptune will sweep you away into the heights."

"That's why you are here. To prepare me for Neptune's crossing. I feel so free with you here," I tell Saturn.

"Right on man!" exclaims Uranus. "Right on! Right on!"

"Lesson five," expostulates Saturn, "is the lesson of limits. When you discover your law, when you discover your truth, you affirm it. You affirm it by saying NO to other options, other truths that would prevent you from realizing the one your Self has chosen. For the power of your NO is the power of your YES to the laws of your being, and to abide by your laws, you must set limits."

"I have tried to be everything, everyone," I say to Saturn. "Jupiter, my 9th house - they grow, they expand in all directions. But I am learning which direction accords with my inner law."

"You are learning to abide by the laws of your being," replies Saturn. "You are discovering your task. Once you discover your task, you must build your center around it. You must organize your Self around an inner foundation, a structure, a solid base from which you act. Only then can you maintain your balance. Only then are you free."

"Jus' look at 'lectricity!" Uranus sparks with excitement. "Your whole body, man, and the whole world 'round you and 'lectricity too, it's about protons and 'lectrons and how they're balanced. Those 'lectrons, man, they whirl in rings round a center. Them rings is their limits and their structure. They make you alive, man, and they give you light. I know," he grins broadly, "'cause not only Saturn's got rings. I got rings too."

"Your rings are your limits," lectures Saturn. "As you discover the essential in your life, you develop rings to

229

*close off the inessential. The lesson of limits is the
lesson of closure-"*

*"'Lectricity needs a closed circuit," interrupts Ura-
nus, "or you don't get no light. If you wanna be open to
the light, man, you gotta keep your feet on the ground so
the light don't burn you, and you gotta close your circuits ev'ry now and then, man, to keep that light goin'.
'Cause it can get dark if you take in ev'rything 'round
you, man, real dark."*

*"Even with people," continues Saturn. "you must know
how to close. You must organize yourself around your center. For only then can you open when you choose to open
and only then can you be a source of light."*

"Once I was told I was like a flower beginning to op-
en. Since then I have opened. Now I must also learn to
close."

*"Even a flower must close its petals," explains Sat-
urn. "If it is to remain a flower."*

"If it's gonna keep wakin' to the light," adds Uranus.

*"For only with limits and closure can you organize the
truth of your being. Only by organizing it can you solidify it. Only by solidifying it can you express it con-
cretely in the world. The lesson of limits leads to the
lessons of concentration and accomplishment," lectures
Saturn. "For what is a truth if you do not live it, a law
if you do not abide by it and a center in yourself if you
do not direct that center outside yourself to fulfill
your task in the world?"*

"I am learning. I learn slowly. This year I narrowed
the realms of my life to the essentials. My center awakened and the Self emerged and directed all my planetary
selves. They committed themselves to one task. Through
this one task, I solidify my center, I make my truth concrete, I re-establish my connection with myself and with
the world."

"You begin to learn lesson six," acknowledges Saturn.

the lesson of commitment. There is commitment to a task and commitment to a person. To commit yourself to a person, you must know when not to commit and when to break free of unviable commitments. But no commitment that the Self makes will be unviable because the Self will teach you the lesson of patience and the lesson of waiting."

"To wait," continues Saturn, "is not to remain passive or to neglect your task because you are involved in the process of looking. To wait means to be committed to your task, knowing that such commitment in time will lead you to people following similar tasks - tasks which their Self has chosen. Only with such people can Self meet Self. Only when Self meets Self is a commitment truly viable. In a viable commitment," expounds Saturn, "two people are committed not to each other, but to the larger Self that encompasses each of their Selves, and to the larger Task which they two share in common."

Uranus is silent throughout Saturn's lecture. He fiddles with the levers of Saturn's electric chair, increasing and decreasing the voltage, attempting to jolt Saturn's equanimity. But instead, he himself is jolted.

"Man!" he exclaims. "That's what real freedom is, man. It ain't runnin' out there lookin' for excitement. 'Cause if you just go out and do your thing and ever'body does their thing to you, man, it's tough, 'cause then you gotta deal with all them problems of do your own thingin' and that dealin' takes you away from your task. But if two people meet and they got freedom in themselves, the freedom that comes from listenin' to their Self and doin' their task, then they're gonna be loyal and r'spons'ble and r'liable with each other 'cause they know that that makes each of them freer to follow their Self. And the more they follow their Self, man, the more Self they got, and the more Self they got, the more Self they got to meet each other with, and the more their Selves meet, man," Uranus zaps his electronic tommy gun straight up in the air, and its light illumines him and Saturn and myself. "There ain't no words in my vocab'lary to tell you just what light there is."

"But it's gotta be the right person," proclaims Uranus. "And that may mean a lot'o waiting. And it's gotta

231

be the Self and not just one of us planets your Self meets. Not even Uranus. You don't need any Uranus out there, man, unless you meet some dude who's got a Uranus like me. But you don't need even that, man," adds Uranus. "'Cause you got me right here."

"I own you now," I tell Uranus. "I change. I express you in my 1st house. I ain't no wishy washy Libra no more. I'm strong. I'm tough. I'm free. I'm my own person."

I turn to Saturn. "I have learned much about the lesson of commitment," I tell him. "but I have in the past been so eager for excitement and so eager for commitment that I never listened to the voice of the Self. I haven't learned the lesson of waiting."

"I learn it now," I tell them. "It is not merely that I am willing to wait. It is that I myself am enough, that I am full, that I am whole. What I want from outside myself, I have now within myself. Where I want to be, I am. Where I want to go, I am already there."

"You are gaining power in your 1st house," informs Saturn. "Do not be afraid of that power. Do not give it away because you fear it. Such power can make even the heights solid and substantial. Power," teaches Saturn, "is not a force to wield over others, for such use of power is truly a lack of power, and not power at all. Power awakens the Self in you and the Self in people around you."

"Power," continues Saturn, "is the gift I give you upon my Return, not because you do not have it, for you have it now, but because you are willing to own it, live it, share it with the world."

"In a year my Return will end. Do not depend upon it for the key to your power. I will always be with you. Uranus will always be with you. But do not attribute to us your power. You are your Self and not merely your planets. You are your own source of power. You are your own source of light."

"Yeah man!" adds Uranus. "You are your own liberation."

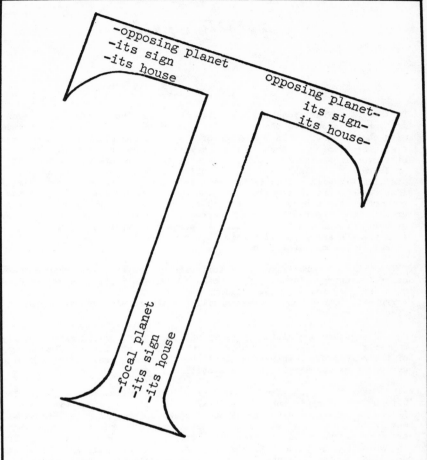

This is your t-square.

It is your weakness and your strength, your vice and your virtue, the source of your conflicts and the indicator of your pathway to growth and achievement.

It is your power and motivation, your inspiration and liberation, the gateway to the Self which links you to other Selves, attunes you to universal wisdom, and enables you to direct all your planetary energies.

Use it. Love it. Respect it. Treat it tenderly. It is you, and you are BEAUTIFUL.

APPENDIX

THE STELLIUM

DEFINITION - Traditionally, a stellium must involve at least four planets (or at least five planets if the Sun, Mercury and Venus are included) with each planet within 8 degrees of the next, and all within the same sign. The meaning of the stellium, however, holds true for any four planets, even if three are interior planets, or if all are within the same house rather than the same sign. Configurations will function like a stellium but with not quite the same intensity if: three rather than four planets are in close conjunction; four planets are in conjunction but not within the same sign or house; orbs between two of the planets are slightly greater than eight degrees; or three planets conjunct a node or angle of the chart. A stellium is particularly strong if more than four planets are involved within it, or if one is the Sun or Moon or a planet in its own sign or house.

INTERPRETATION - Positive characteristics of the stellium include: concentrated energy, focus, genius, talent, self-motivation, sense of direction and purpose, and singlemindedness. Negative characteristics include: narrowness, obsession, over-emphasis, imbalance, self-centeredness, difficulty compromising, and lack of objectivity.

Planets in a stellium normally act as a unit, giving extraordinary emphasis to the sign and/or house in which they are placed. The meaning of the sign/house combination should be interpreted before the individual conjunctions contained within the stellium.

Consider the stellium to be like a close family. If the father loses his job, everyone in the family is affected. If a daughter wins an award in school, everyone experiences her happiness. In a stellium, those planets which are closest will most affect each other, but even those which are more distant will experience the repercussions. Usually, the planet in the middle or closest to the midpoint of the stellium will be the most sensitive to the influences of the other planets.

Aspects the stellium makes to other planets or to the angles of the chart will indicate how the stellium functions in relation to other energies in the chart. Because transits and progressions create a chain reaction which triggers all the planets within the stellium, people with stelliums will experience periods of calm in their lives alternating with periods of intense upheaval and change.

THE GRAND TRINE

DEFINITION - The grand trine involves three planets, usually in the same element, in trine to each other - the first trine the second, the second trine the third, and the third trine the first. A grand trine is strong if it involves more than three planets in the same element and weak if it involves more than one element.

INTERPRETATION - Positive characteristics of a grand trine include: free energy flow, luck, ease in obtaining benefits and opportunities, self-motivation, self-sufficiency and talent - all related to one particular element. Negative characteristics include: laziness, inertia, escapism or avoidance of challenge, "moving in circles", bound by habits or past patterns of behavior, closed, distant, living in "one's own world".

Grand trines have been best described by Noel Tyl, who refers to them as "closed circuits of self-sufficiency". People with grand trines are motivated, independent and talented when functioning on the level of the element emphasized by their grand trine, but tend to "get stuck" or to retreat into that one part of themselves. A person with a grand fire trine will have ceaseless energy and vitality but will have difficulty slowing down, understanding another person's point of view, or channelling energy in response to another person's needs. A person with a grand air trine may be intellectually and socially a world to himself, able to provide his own mental stimulation, but often unable to turn off his mind and deal directly with emotional or practical issues. A person with a grand earth trine will be able to apply himself successfully to a job and will easily attract and manage material resources, but may become bound by ambition or mundane concerns and closed to other sources of meaning in his life. A person with a grand water trine will have an active emotional life and a high degree of sensitivity, but may be unable to share his feelings with other people or rise above his feelings and view himself objectively.

When interpreting a grand trine, consider not only the element which the grand trine accentuates, but also the nature of the planets and houses involved in the configuration. If one planet in the grand trine is also a pivotal planet, linking the grand trine to another aspect configuration, that planet will be the key to effectively expressing the talents of both configurations. The closest square or opposition to a grand trine is also important, for it is the spark of motivation which aids a person in applying his fire, earth, air or water talents to other areas of his life. A grand trine with an opposition to one of its planets is called a kite formation; the opposing planet can lead to increased awareness, and is a powerful channel for the expression of grand trine energies.

THE YOD OR FINGER OF GOD

DEFINITION - The yod consists of two planets in sextile, each inconjuncting (150 degrees) a third planet, located at the far midpoint of the sextile. No orbs are more than five degrees. The planet which receives both inconjuncts is the focal or action planet.

INTERPRETATION - The yod configuration calls for emotional or mental readjustment and regeneration. The focal planet indicates the energies which must be regenerated; its sign, the way in which they need to be corrected or re-experienced; and its house, the area of life through which this transformation will take place. The focal planet is a very sensitive planet because its inconjuncts (6th and 8th house aspects) create a subliminal tension which can result in physical or psychological problems. This planet has been referred to as the mission in life, the finger of God, the finger of fate, the ultimate destiny, and the celestial pointer. Its negative manifestations must be cast out, as one casts out devils, and its highest expression activated. As the far midpoint of the sextile, it is the mediator which can use the dynamic creative energy and opportunity presented by the sextile to bring about a new way of being; it is the point of transmutation in the chart, the alchemical agent which can create an entirely new pattern of thinking and feeling.

People with yods generally experience turning points in their lives during which they confront a crisis and resolve it through a change in consciousness, often experienced as a seemingly fated change in life direction. This transformation at its best leads to increased spiritual sensitivity and awareness, the flowing of new energies, the building of an inner center, and the discovery of a concrete means for expressing one's creativity. Yods with a planet at the near midpoint of the sextile (30 degrees from each planet in sextile) are called tetradic yods, and especially require a transformation leading to concrete action and the practical expression of creativity.

THE GRAND CROSS (OR COSMIC CROSS)

DEFINITION - The grand cross consists of at least four planets, four squares and two oppositions. The first planet squares the second, the second squares the third, the third squares the fourth, and the fourth squares the first. Oppositions link the first and third planets as well as the second and fourth planets. Generally, all planets are in signs of the same mode, and orbs do not exceed eight degrees.

Weaker variations of the grand cross involve planets in a combination of two modes (such as cardinal and mutable) or one planet slightly out of orb (10 - 12 degrees). Configurations which are created by an opposition in square to the nodes, ascendant/descendant axis or the M.C./ I.C. axis may function somewhat in the manner of a weak grand cross.

INTERPRETATION - Positive characteristics of a grand cross include inner power and strength, determination, the will to fulfill a purpose, productivity, concentration and channelling of diverse energies, and the ability to integrate all dimensions of one's experience and translate ideals and values into concrete form. Negative characteristics include stagnation, inertia, scattering of energies, tremendous inner tension, resignation, the Atlas syndrome (carrying the weight of the world) and self-defeating behavior.

People with grand crosses generally feel pulled in four directions, and overburdened by the demands which they, as well as other people, place upon their time and energy. They live as if trapped in a room with four locked doors, and frequently try to force each door open by pounding upon it until they have exhausted themselves. Yet their situation is not hopeless, for if they position themselves in the middle of the room, they will discover a central staircase which will lead them to the roof and open air.

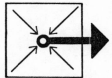

from scatteredness   to centeredness   to centered action

These people often feel stuck, paralyzed by the problems in their lives which seem to be unresolvable, until they turn inward and discover their own inner center – until they are able to attain a spiritual or creative state of consciousness which allows them to rise above their mundane conflicts and view their life with clarity and objectivity. They need to examine the polarities in their lives, integrating and synthesizing seemingly contradictory facets of their experience (signified by the planets, signs and houses which oppose each other) around a purpose or goal which takes all parts of themselves into consideration. They need to concentrate their energy, and direct it outward to fulfill the goal they have chosen. Evaluation, concentration, integration and application are the lessons to be learned from the grand cross.

When interpreting a grand cross, pay attention to the nature of the planets involved, their mode, and the houses in which they are placed in the chart. The opposition or square with the smallest orb will be a key to the most pressing problem in regard to awareness or action, and must be resolved if energies are to be collected and focused effectively. Look also to the closest trine or sextile to planets in the cross, for the planet making the trine or sextile (and sometimes even a quintile) will be important in helping the individual to clarify his/her life situation and find a meaningful channel for his/her scattered energy.

The difficulties presented by a cross are related to the mode in which it occurs; the resolutions of its conflicts must be through that particular mode, which indicates a person's talents as well as his problems. A person with a cardinal cross needs to involve himself in activities of personal importance, but because he is an over-doer and may scatter himself in too many directions in a frantic manner, he has to learn to focus his energies before plunging into action. A person with a fixed cross slowly builds up a high degree of inner tension, due to frustrated needs and desires, and then powerfully explodes into forceful and sometimes destructive action; he is strong-willed, stubborn and can be extremely productive, provided that he find outlets through which he can constructively release his pent-up energy. A person with a mutable cross is likely to be so easily influenced by his relationships and external circumstances that he tends, like a chameleon, to alter himself to suit his changing environment; he needs to define his identity – his needs, desires, goals, and to act in a manner that is true to himself while maintaining a satisfying network of personal relationships.

BOOKS BY TRACY MARKS

THE ASTROLOGY OF SELF-DISCOVERY: An In-depth Exploration of the Potentials Revealed in Your Birth Chart . . . 288-page paperback, packed with information!. **$9.95**
A guide to utilizing astrology to aid self-development and self-knowledge, to resolve inner conflicts, discover and fulfill one's life purpose, and to realize one's potential. Emphasizes the Moon and its nodes, Neptune, Pluto, and the outer planets' transits. An important and original work!

THE ART OF CHART INTERPRETATION: A Step-by-Step Method of Analyzing, Synthesizing & Understanding the Birth Chart . . . 180-page paperback . . . a must for students!. **$7.95**
A great value and a great book, this is a revised, expanded version of the author's book on Chart Synthesis. It is a guide for determining the most important features of any birth chart; there is no book like it! Includes worksheets that allow the reader to systematically evaluate the patterns and themes of any chart.

PLANETARY ASPECTS—FROM CONFLICT TO COOPERATION: How to Make Your Stressful Aspects Work for You . . . 228-page paperback . . . a best-selling classic!. **$11.95**
This new edition of *How to Handle Your T-Square* focuses on the creative understanding and use of the stressful aspects and emphasizes the T-Square Configuration both in natal charts and as formed by transits and progressions. The most thorough treatment of these subjects in print! Includes techniques for handling these challenges.

YOUR SECRET SELF: Illuminating the Mysteries of the Twelfth House . . . 264 pages. **$12.95**
The most comprehensive treatment of the 12th House and its subtleties ever published. The importance of the 12th House for self-knowledge and the dimensions of psychological and spiritual potential that it symbolizes are emphasized. It also demonstrates in a fascinating way how the themes of a birth chart emerge in one's dreams and how working with dreams is one of the most effective gateways into the hidden meanings of the 12th House.

CRCS PUBLICATIONS

ASTROLOGY, PSYCHOLOGY & THE FOUR ELEMENTS: An Energy Approach to Astrology & Its Use in the Counseling Arts by Stephen Arroyo .... $7.95 Paperback; $14.95 Hardcover
An international best-seller, this book deals with the relation of astrology to modern psychology and with the use of astrology as a practical method of understanding one's attunement to universal forces. Clearly shows how to approach astrology with a real understanding of the energies involved. Awarded the British Astrological Assn's. Astrology Prize. A classic translated into 8 languages!

ASTROLOGY AND THE MODERN PSYCHE: An Astrologer Looks at Depth Psychology by Dane Rudhyar .... 182 pages, Paperback $8.95
Deals with Depth-Psychology's pioneers with special emphasis on Jung's concepts related to astrology. Chapters on: Psychodrama, Psychosynthesis, Sex Factors in Personality, the Astrologer's Role as Consultant.

ASTROLOGY, KARMA, & TRANSFORMATION: The Inner Dimensions of the Birth-Chart by Stephen Arroyo .... 264 pages, 10.95 Paperback; $17.95 Deluxe Sewn Hardcover
An insightful book on the use of astrology as a tool for spiritual and psychological growth, seen in the light of the theory of karma and the urge toward self-transformation. International best-seller.

CYCLES OF BECOMING: The Planetary Pattern of Growth by Alexander Ruperti .... 6 x 9 Paperback, 274 pages, $12.50
The first complete treatment of transits from a humanistic and holistic perspective. All important planetary cycles are correlated with the essential phases of psychological development. A pioneering work!

AN ASTROLOGICAL GUIDE TO SELF-AWARENESS by Donna Cunningham, M.S.W. .... 210 pages, Paperback $6.95
Written in a lively style by a social worker who uses astrology in counseling, this book includes chapters on transits, houses, interpreting aspects, etc. A popular book translated into 3 languages.

RELATIONSHIPS & LIFE CYCLES: Modern Dimensions of Astrology by Stephen Arroyo .... 228 pages, Paperback $7.95
A collection of articles and workshops on: natal chart indicators of one's capacity and need for relationship; techniques of chart comparison; using transits practically; counseling; and the use of the houses in chart comparison.

REINCARNATION THROUGH THE ZODIAC by Joan Hodgson ..... Paperback $5.50
A study of the signs of the zodiac from a spiritual perspective, based upon the development of different phases of consciousness through reincarnation. First published in England as *Wisdom in the Stars*.

LOOKING AT ASTROLOGY by Liz Greene .... 8½ x 11, $6.95
A beautiful, full-color children's book for ages 6-13. Illustrated by the author, this is the best explanation of astrology for children and was highly recommended by *School Library Journal*. It emphasizes a healthy self-acceptance and a realistic understanding of others. A beautiful gift for children or for your local library.

A SPIRITUAL APPROACH TO ASTROLOGY by Myrna Lofthus ... Paperback $12.50
A complete astrology textbook from a karmic viewpoint, with an especially valuable 130-page section on karmic interpretations of all aspects, including the Ascendant & M.C. A huge 444-page, highly original work.

THE ASTROLOGER'S GUIDE TO COUNSELING: Astrology's Role in the Helping Professions by Bernard Rosenblum, M.D. .... Paperback $7.95
Establishes astrological counseling as a valid, valuable, and legitimate helping profession, which can also be beneficially used in conjunction with other therapeutic and healing arts.

THE JUPITER/SATURN CONFERENCE LECTURES *(Lectures on Modern Astrology Series)* by Stephen Arroyo & Liz Greene .... Paperback $8.95
Transcribed from lectures given under the 1981 Jupiter, Saturn Conjunction, talks included deal with myth, chart synthesis, relationships, & Jungian psychology related to astrology.

THE OUTER PLANETS & THEIR CYCLES: The Astrology of the Collective *(Lectures on Modern Astrology Series)* by Liz Greene .... Paperback $7.95
Deals with the individual's attunement to the outer planets as well as with significant historical and generational trends that correlate to these planetary cycles.

CHILD SIGNS: Understanding Your Child Through Astrology by Dodie & Allan Edmands 150 pages, 12 photos of children .... Paperback $7.95
An in-depth treatment of a child's developmental psychology from an astrological viewpoint. Recommended by *Library Journal*, this book helps parents understand and appreciate their children more fully. Nice gift!

DYNAMICS OF ASPECT ANALYSIS: New Perceptions in Astrology by Bil Tierney. Groundbreaking new work! .... 288 pages, Paperback $8.95
The most in-depth treatment of aspects and aspect patterns available, including both major and minor configurations. Also includes retrogrades, unaspected planets & more!

ASTROLOGY FOR THE NEW AGE: An Intuitive Approach by Marcus Allen .... Paperback $6.95
A highly original work with an uplifting quality. Emphasizes self-acceptance and tuning in to your own birth chart with a positive attitude. Helps one create his or her own interpretation.

THE PRACTICE & PROFESSION OF ASTROLOGY: Rebuilding Our Lost Connections with the Cosmos by Stephen Arroyo .... Paperback $7.95
A challenging, often controversial treatment of astrology's place in modern society and of astrological counseling as both a legitimate profession and a healing process.

HEALTH-BUILDING: The Conscious Art of Living Well by Dr. Randolph Stone, D.C., D.O. Approx. 150 pages, Paperback $7.95
A complete health regimen for people of all ages by an internationally renowned doctor who specialized in problem cases. Includes instructions for vegetarian/purifying diets and energizing exercises for vitality and beauty. Illustrated with drawings & photographs.